Piano · Vocal · Guitar

2ND EDITION

THE YIP HARBURG SONGBOOK

ISBN: 978-1-4234-8282-6

HAL·LEONARD® CORPORATION

7777 W. BLUEMOUND RD. P.O. BOX 13819 MILWAUKEE, WI 53213

Visit Hal Leonard Online at
www.halleonard.com

CONTENTS

THE LYRICS OF YIP HARBURG

BY STEPHEN HOLDEN

(©1993 reprinted)

L to R: "Chorus Girls", dance director Bobby Connolly, composer Jay Gorney, lyricist Yip Harburg on the set of Universal's film musical <u>Moonlight and Pretzels</u> (1933). *Courtesy Harburg Estate.*

George and Ira Gershwin, Beverly Hills, 1937, inscribed to Yip. *Courtesy Harburg Estate.*

When E.Y. ("Yip") Harburg died in 1981, American music lost a song lyricist whose mixture of compassion, humor, conscience and craft were well ahead of their time. The man who wrote the words for "Brother, Can You Spare a Dime?" and "Over the Rainbow" was a social realist who believed in a better world, a romantic who saw through his own illusions, a man of the people who was a master of the sophisticated bon mot, a skeptic who had faith. If these qualities seem contradictory, they were reconciled in Harburg's lyrics by an expansive sense of humor and an unshakeable faith in human nature. If Harburg could accept a paper moon in a cardboard sky and still believe in love, he reasoned, so could everybody else. Life might indeed be a joke, but it was still a delicious one.

It is widely and mistakenly believed that social relevance only entered the mainstream of American song with the folk music boom of the 1950s and 60s and became entrenched during the heyday of the rock counterculture. This assumption disregards the satirical operettas of George and Ira Gershwin. It ignores the racial issues in shows from *Show Boat* to *South Pacific*. Most significantly, it overlooks the work of Yip Harburg, a lyricist who, more than sixty years ago, identified with the common man as passionately and persuasively as songwriters like Bruce Springsteen and Tom Waits do today.

Harburg's very first hit, "Brother, Can You Spare a Dime?" swept the country in 1932 and became a kind of theme song for the Depression. Some even credit it with helping to elect Franklin D. Roosevelt president. Listening to it now, you can't help but be struck by the similarities between Harburg and Springsteen. Harburg's narrator, who fought for his country in World War I but can't find a job, is a direct forerunner of the unemployed Vietnam veteran who howls his frustration and bitterness in Springsteen's "Born in the U.S.A." Tom Waits' rendition of the "Dime" song in 1993 cries out for the homeless in these times.

Harburg went on to write lyrics for a number of Broadway musicals, all with strong political messages, two of which were big hits. His 1944 show, *Bloomer Girl*, which had music by Harold Arlen, was set in the 1860s and exalted feminism and black civil rights with an understated but clear anti-war current running throughout. His 1947 show and biggest success, *Finian's Rainbow*, with music by Burton Lane (and book by Harburg and Fred Saidy), satirized American materialism in its story of a naive Irish immigrant who buries a crock of gold in the hope that it will grow and make him rich. The show also attacked racism satirically: a bigoted white Senator is turned black to see how it feels. *Finian* was one of the first Broadway shows in which black and white actors danced together in the chorus as equals, largely due to Harburg's efforts. Among its gems are the meltingly lyrical "How Are Things in Glocca Morra," the sultry "Old Devil Moon" and the wistful "Look to the Rainbow" (one of three Harburg songs with rainbows in their titles)

The show's satiric masterpiece, "When the Idle Poor Become the Idle Rich," is as scalding a social critique as any contemporary rap diatribe. A modified patter song, it offers an analysis of the relationship of wealth, morality, and public perception that is as witty as it is devastating:

"When a rich man doesn't want to work,
He's a bon vivant,
Yes, he's a bon vivant.
But when a poor man doesn't want to work,
He's a loafer, he's a lounger,
He's a lazy good for nothing, he's a jerk."

Earl Robinson. *Courtesy Harburg Estate.*

Harold Arlen (w/dog) and Yip at work in Beverly Hills.
Courtesy Harburg Estate.

Harburg's most famous lyrics, written with composer Harold Arlen, were for the 1939 film classic, *The Wizard of Oz*. While not generally thought of as socially relevant, it can be seen as an allegorical meditation on the Depression and society's loss of faith in itself, expressed in a language that brilliantly melded rose-colored Hollywood sentiments with a Gilbert-and-Sullivanesque wit. And Harburg's

Harold Arlen posing with his dog. Inscribed to Yip.
Courtesy Harburg Estate.

Harold Arlen and Yip at work. *Credit: ASCAP*

wonderfully idiosyncratic yet universal lyrics for the Scarecrow, the Tin Man, and the Cowardly Lion's comic laments are supreme examples of lyrics that define the characters who inspire them. Though uncredited, Harburg also wrote all of the dialogue in the long song sequences and edited the final script.

The score's most famous song, of course, is "Over the Rainbow," which countless pop divas and a number of male singers have inflated into a grandiose aria of romantic yearning. Today, when the song is identified with a top pop gospel belter, it is easy to forget that "Over the Rainbow" originated as a wistful expression of hope in hard times sung by a Kansas farm girl (the young Judy Garland). It is a measure of the song's greatness that whether confided softly to an ominous Kansas sky or belted as a stentorian pop-soul anthem, its lyric still has a universal ring. Indeed, it is a global song.

Even though Harburg has yet to become a household name like Irving Berlin or Cole Porter, he is in fact among the songwriters whom Alec Wilder christened "the great craftsmen" of American popular song. One reason why he remains so underappreciated is that his name was never linked indelibly to a composer in the way that Lorenz Hart and Oscar Hammerstein II became joined at the hip to Richard Rodgers, or Alan J. Lerner to Frederick Loewe, or Ira Gershwin to his

brother George. Although Harold Arlen was Harburg's most important collaborator (they wrote over 100 songs together), he and Arlen each did enough significant work with others to prevent them from being thought of as rock-solid partners.

Among the two dozen or so songwriters who embodied the craftsmanly pre-rock tradition, however, Harburg was alone in expressing through the prism of a lyric, a singular philosophic version of the world. Irving Berlin had a knack for sensing the mood of the country and distilling it in a snappy all-American vernacular. Ira Gershwin sketched pictures of New York that wittily conveyed the vitality of the melting pot. Cole Porter offered particular insights into sexual passion and the manners of high society. Lorenz Hart was pop's most graceful poet of loneliness and vulnerability while Oscar Hammerstein II's lyrics crystallized a middle-class dream of stability and moral uplift. Yip Harburg's lyrics reflect his belief that art should be rooted in the struggle for survival and that songs should empower people with courage, reality and hope in that struggle.

Harburg's gift was a brilliantly focused double vision. He saw the world with a levelling but loving eye. The world might be cruel and existence absurd, his lyrics suggested, but somewhere at the end of it all, there really was a rainbow. For all his bitterness, the narrator of "Brother, Can You Spare a Dime?" could still address a fellow countryman as "brother," and also ask the profound question, "Why should

I be standing in line just waiting for bread?" In "It's Only a Paper Moon," which he wrote in 1933 with Arlen (Billy Rose also has a questionable credit), he deals with existential questions. Without an act of faith, the lyric asserts, the universe is a tawdry, worthless fake.

"It's a Barnum and Bailey world
Just as phony as it can be
But it wouldn't be make-believe
If you believed in me."

Part of its brilliance is the way the lyric expresses such heavyweight apprehensions in a breezy, lighter-than-air language. In Harburg's lyrics it wasn't inconsistent for a heartfelt populism to coincide with an aesthetic elegance. The precision and polish of his finest patter songs matched those of his idol, W.S. Gilbert. But at the same time, he translated Gilbert's frivolity into a plainer American vernacular that for all its playfulness avoided unnecessary frills and still was able to "gild the philosophic pill." He was also a master of the O. Henry last liner.

Yip at work. *Courtesy Harburg Estate*

This realist with a rainbow vision, who wrote lyrics for over 500 songs, was born in poverty on the Lower East Side of Manhattan in 1896, the same year as his schoolmate and lifelong friend Ira Gershwin. As youths the two contributed humorous pieces to their high school and City College newspapers. After a short stint as co-owner of an electric appliance business, Harburg turned to songwriting under the tutelage of Ira Gershwin and Jay Gorney (who wrote the music for "Brother, Can You Spare a Dime?"). One of his great early successes was "April in Paris," an eternal salute to a city he had never visited, with music by Vernon Duke.

Through the 1930s, Harburg wrote lyrics for various Broadway revues, the most successful being the 1937 anti-war satire *Hooray for What!*, which he conceived, with music by Arlen.

After *The Wizard of Oz*, the most significant milestone in his film career were his lyrics, again with music by Arlen, for the film version of Broadway's first all-black musical, *Cabin in the Sky*, in which Ethel Waters introduced "Happiness Is a Thing Called Joe."

Returning to Broadway, he wrote the lyrics for *BloomerGirl,* which he also co-directed. Four other shows followed: *Flahooley* (1951, with music by Sammy Fain), *Jamaica* (1957, music by Arlen), *The Happiest Girl in the World* (1961, music adapted from Offenbach), and *Darling of the Day* (1968, music by Jule Styne). Each had a satiric social message. *Flahooley* lampooned the dire consequences of overproduction for American consumerism. *Jamaica*'s score, which laughed at the struggles of love and the transience of fame, also warned early on about the dangers of the atomic bomb. *The Happiest Girl in the World* was an anti-war show based on the Lysistrata story. *Darling of the Day* mocked the British class system.

Four Harburg lyrics that deserve special mention were in songs which he entitled "Last Night When We Were Young," "Lydia, the Tattooed Lady," "Poor You" and "Time, You Old Gypsy Man." Although entirely different from one another in style and mood, each is perfect in its own way. And beneath their dissimilarities, they share the quiet, warm-hearted wisdom that radiated through Harburg's lyrics.

Yip and Burton Lane. *Courtesy Harburg Estate*

Yip and Sammy Fain. *Courtesy Harburg Estate*

Johnny Green. *Courtesy Harburg Estate*

Yip and Fred Saidy. *Courtesy Harburg Estate*

"Last Night When We Were Young," which has music by Arlen, was introduced by Lawrence Tibbett in the mid-1930s. But it wasn't until twenty years later when Frank Sinatra made it the centerpiece of his album, *In the Wee Small Hours*, that it became recognized as one of the most imposing of all torch songs.

Like "It's Only a Paper Moon," the song evokes a world in which life is almost unbearable without love and faith. But here the tone is formal and elegiac:

"Today the world is old
You went away and time grew cold
Where is that star that seemed so bright
Ages ago, last night."

Listening to Sinatra stretch out the word "ages" in a world-weary groan is to be transported for a moment to the center of the earth and to feel the deepest loneliness. "Last Night" was Yip's only major song about an irrevocable loss of love.

"Lydia, the Tattooed Lady," which became Groucho Marx's theme song after he introduced it in the movie *A Day at the Circus*, is a masterpiece of elegantly playful salaciousness. Harburg's lyric to this gallumphing waltz (with a tune by Arlen) offers a hilarious topsy-turvy road map to the historical and mythical lore concealed in the fleshy folds of an undulating circus performer:

"Lydia, oh Lydia
That 'encyclopidia,'
Oh, Lydia, the queen of tattoo.
On her back is the battle of Waterloo
Beside it the wreck of the Hesperus too
And proudly above waves the red, white and blue
You can learn a lot from Lydia."

In "Poor You," Harburg surpassed almost everybody in coming up with a newer and cleverer type of love song. The love-smitten narrator of the ballad, which has music by Burton Lane, laments the fact that his beloved can never experience the joy he feels, she being the object of his adoration:

"When it is you I'm kissing
I pity you constantly
You don't know what you're missing
For you're only kissing poor me."

Two years before his death in 1981, Harburg collaborated with Phil Springer, a moderately successful tune-smith ("How Little We Know"), to write one of the most honest pop songs about aging and mortality. "Time, You Old Gypsy Man" (not included in this edition) takes its title from a verse by the English poet Ralph Hodgson. Here, Harburg imagines Father Time not as the benign bearded figure of children's storybooks, but as a thieving carnival trickster who has stripped him down to nothing.

[You] "whistled the bird of youth out of my skies," accuses the narrator, [and you] "turned off the stars." In the final verse, he even cedes his own creative powers. [You] "took away song and spring/Robbed me of rhyme/Fled in your carnival caravan." Then, in a dazzling verbal pirouette, Harburg turns the song around. "But you old gypsy man," he reflects, "Thanks for a glorious time."

"Glorious" is the one and only word that could turn around such a sad song.

For Harburg's final, unshakeable belief in the preciousness of life is what gave his double vision of what it means to be alive in a Barnum and Bailey world such a special, touching balance.

"Glorious" also describes the singular blend of brains and heart, courage and humor that infuses Harburg's song lyrics. His "elegant legacy" lives on.

To read more about Yip Harburg:
Who Put the Rainbow in the Wizard of Oz?:
Yip Harburg, Lyricist
by Harold Meyerson and Ernie Harburg,
(Ann Arbor: University of Michigan Press, 1993).

ADRIFT ON A STAR

Lyric by E.Y. "YIP" HARBURG
Music by JACQUES OFFENBACH

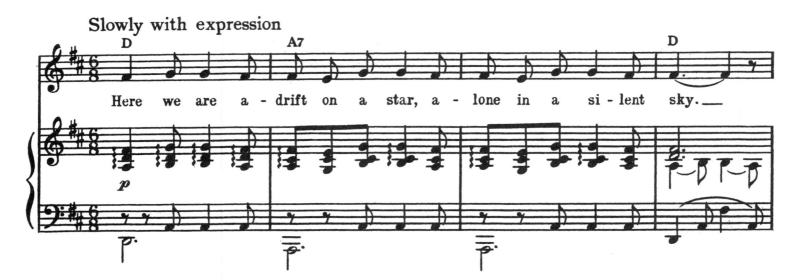

Here we are a-drift on a star, a-lone in a si-lent sky.___

Lost in space, to-geth-er we face the won-der of where and why._

Why a sky with-out an end, a sea with-out a chart?_

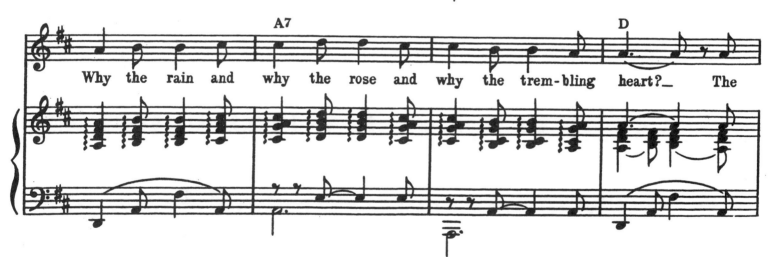

Why the rain and why the rose and why the trem-bling heart?_ The

moon, the tide, the years,_ They go roll-ing a - long._ Oh

mu - sic of the spheres, ___ Are there words to your

song? Is there a bright _____ gleam - ing goal End - ing this

brief _____ bar - ca - rolle? _____

Here we are a - drift on a star And what is the jour - ney for? ____

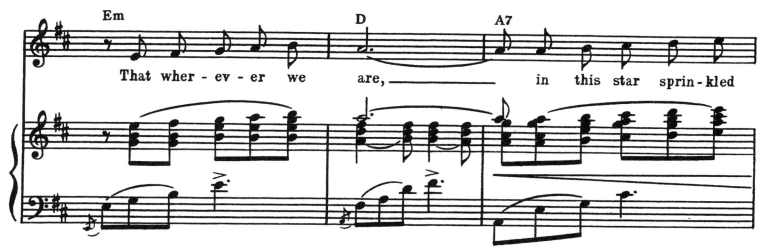

AIN'T IT DE TRUTH

from JAMAICA

Lyric by E.Y. "YIP" HARBURG
Music by HAROLD ARLEN

1. Life is short, short, broth-er! AIN' IT DE TRUTH? An' dere is no oth-er,
2. (Life is) short, short, broth-er! AIN' IT DE TRUTH? An' dere is no oth-er,

AIN' IT DE TRUTH? You got-ta grab dat rain-bow while you still got your youth, Oh!
AIN' IT DE TRUTH? So if you don't love liv-in' you is slight-ly un-couth, Oh!

ain' it de sol-id truth?_____ Was a man called Ad-am,
ain' it de dig-ni-fied truth?_____ Said dat gal Du-bar-ry,

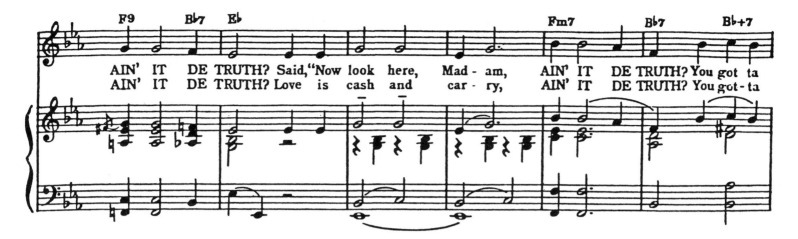

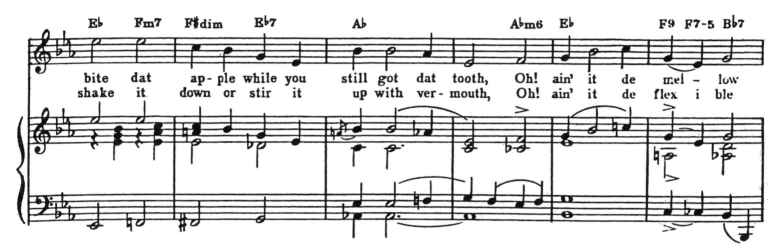

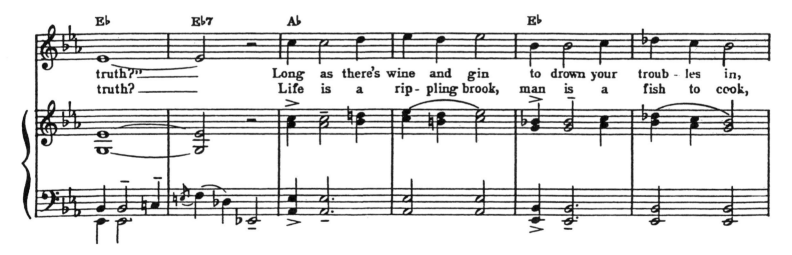

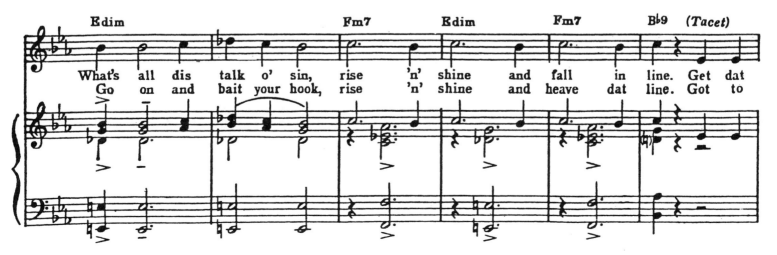

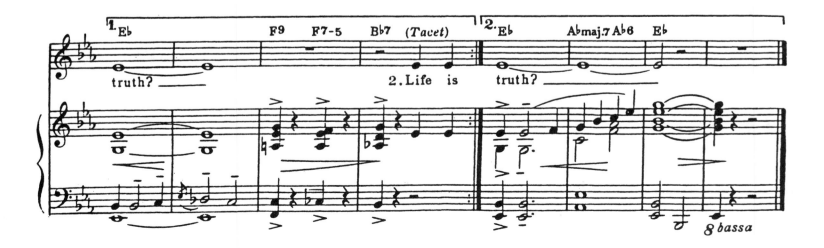

DING-DONG! THE WITCH IS DEAD

from THE WIZARD OF OZ

Lyric by E.Y. "YIP" HARBURG
Music by HAROLD ARLEN

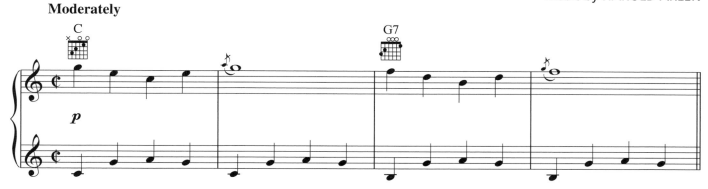

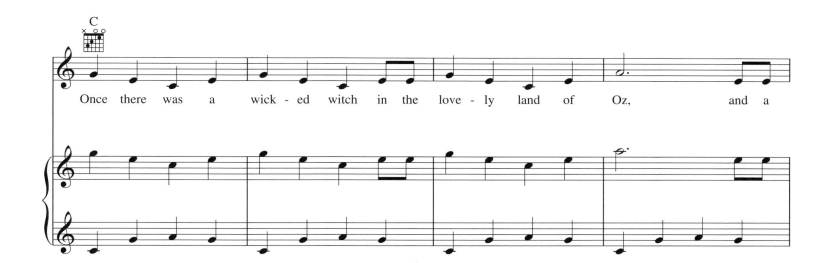

Once there was a wick-ed witch in the love-ly land of Oz, and a

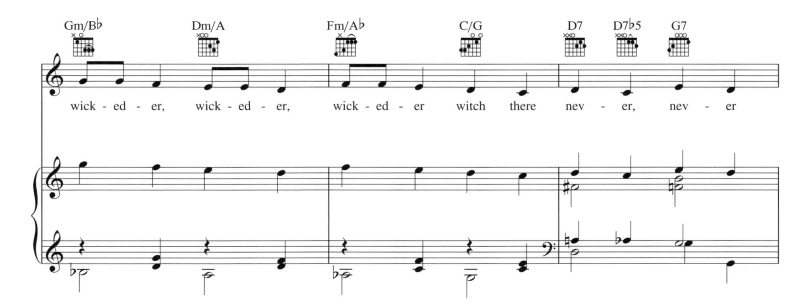

wick-ed-er, wick-ed-er, wick-ed-er witch there nev-er, nev-er

was. She filled the folks in Munch - kin land with ter - ror and with

dread, 'til one fine day from Kan - sas way a cy - clone caught a

poco accel.

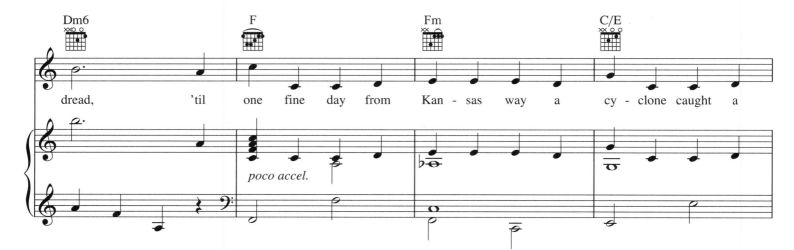

house that brought the wick - ed, wick - ed, witch her doom as she was fly - ing

poco rit.

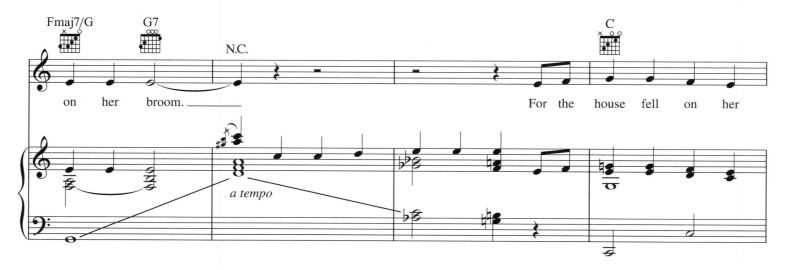

on her broom. _____ For the house fell on her

a tempo

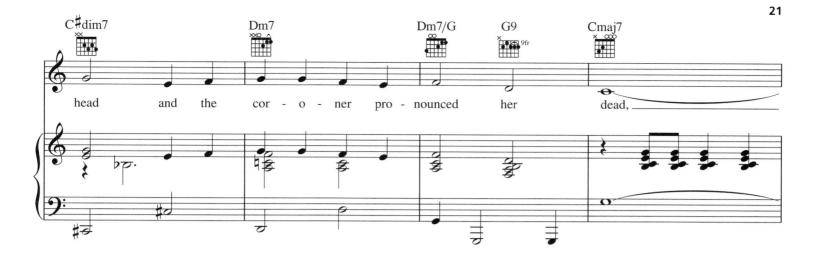

head and the cor-o-ner pro-nounced her dead, ___

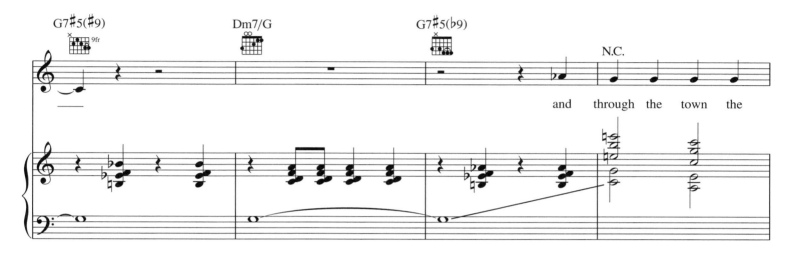

___ and through the town the

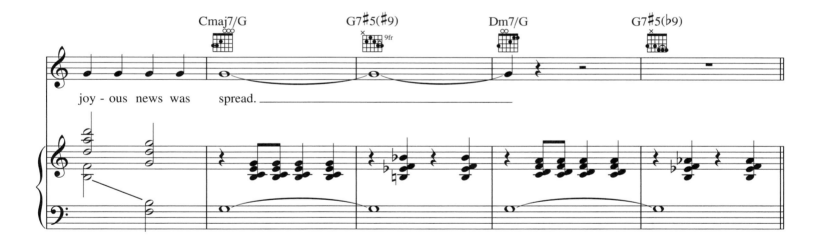

joy-ous news was spread. ___

Ding — dong, the witch is dead! Which old witch? The wick-ed witch.

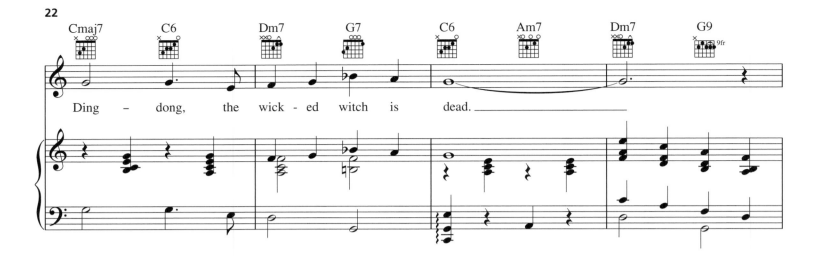

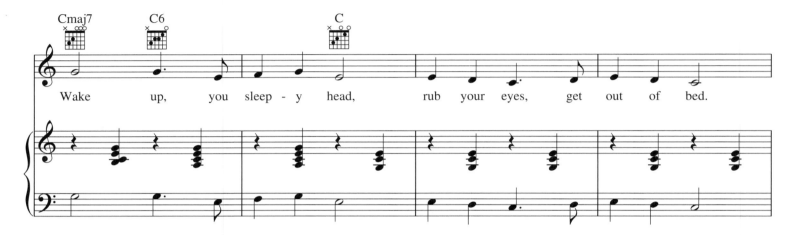

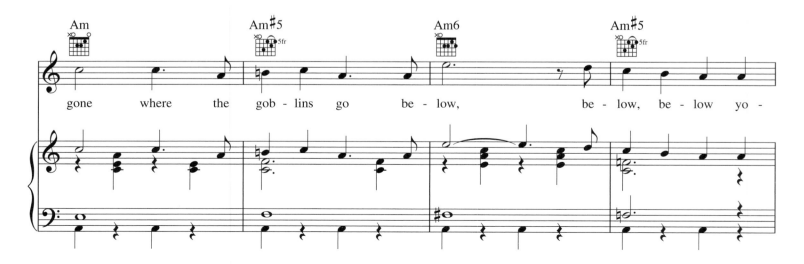

ho let's o - pen up and sing, and ring the bells out:

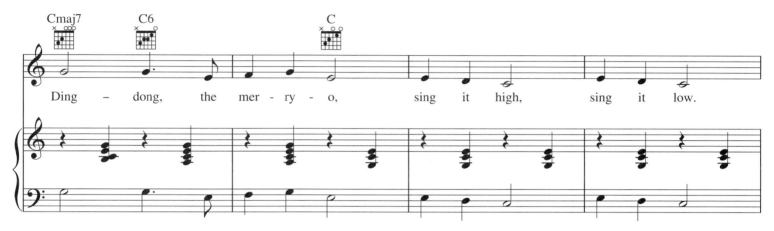

Ding - dong, the mer - ry - o, sing it high, sing it low.

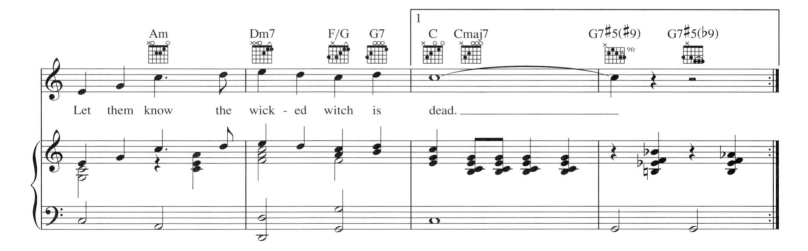

Let them know the wick - ed witch is dead. _____

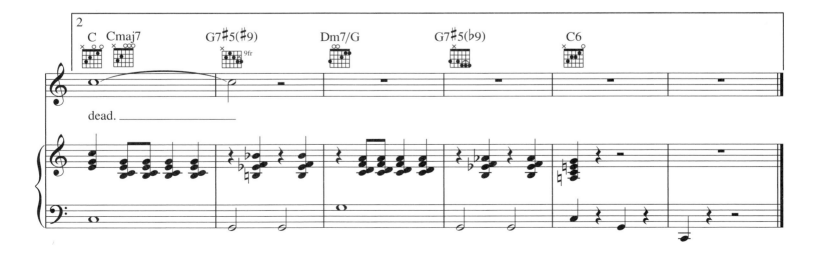

dead. _____

APRIL IN PARIS

Words by E.Y. "YIP" HARBURG
Music by VERNON DUKE

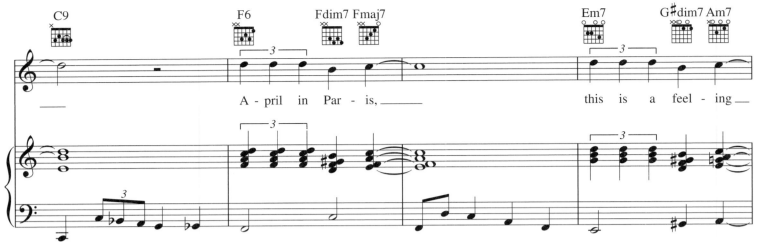

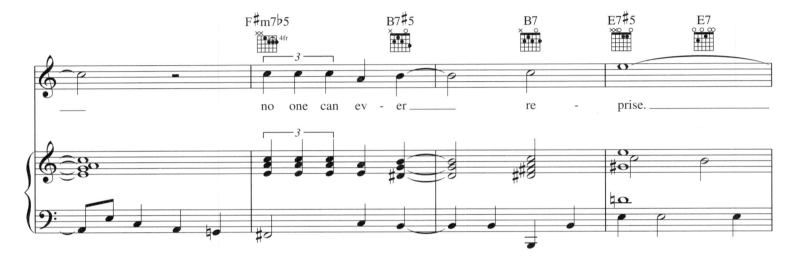

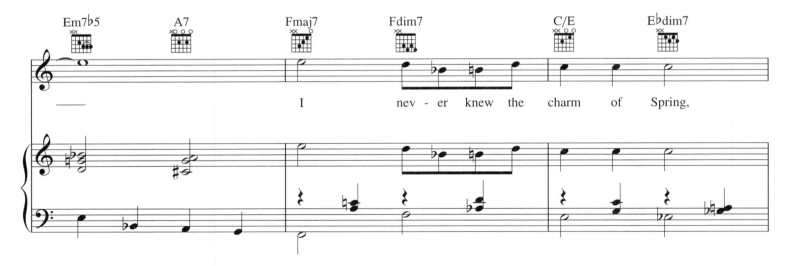

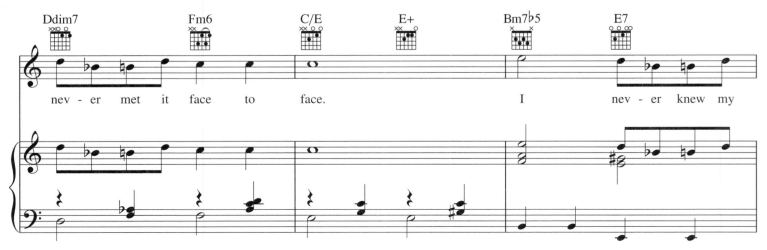

heart could sing, never missed a warm em - brace, till

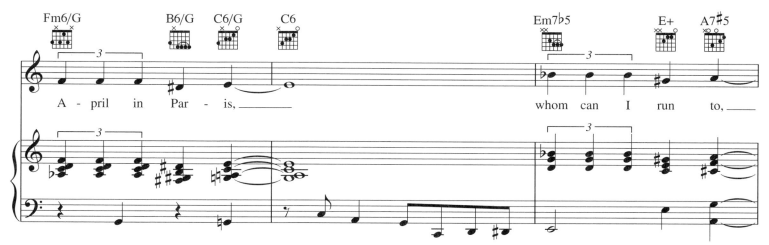

A - pril in Par - is, whom can I run to,

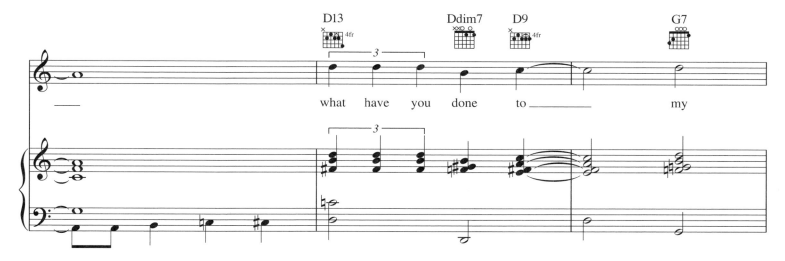

what have you done to my

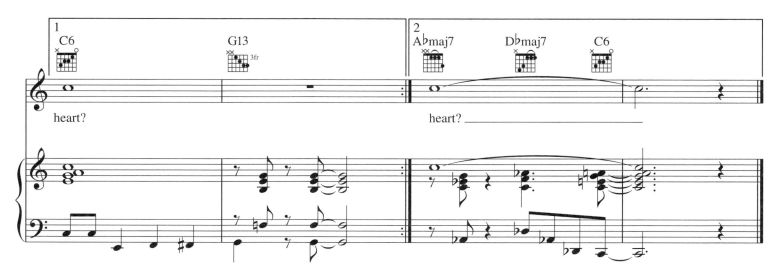

heart? heart?

THE BEGAT

By E.Y. "YIP" HARBURG
and BURTON LANE

ap-ple trees. _____ Then she looked at him, _____ and he looked at

her, _____ and they knew im-med-jet-ly _____ what the world was fur. _____

1st MAN

— He said give me my cane, _____ He said give me my hat, _____ The time has

come to be-gin The Be-Gat. _____ So they

SENATOR

The Be-gat, The Be-gat. So they

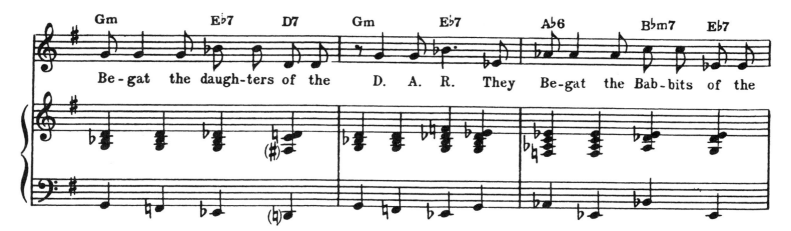

Be-gat the daugh-ters of the D. A. R. They Be-gat the Bab-bits of the

bour-geo-sie, Who Be-gat the mis-be-got-ten V. I. P. —

It was pleas-in' to Jez-e-bel,

pleas-in' to Ruth. It pleased the league of Wo-men Shop-pers in Du-luth. Though the

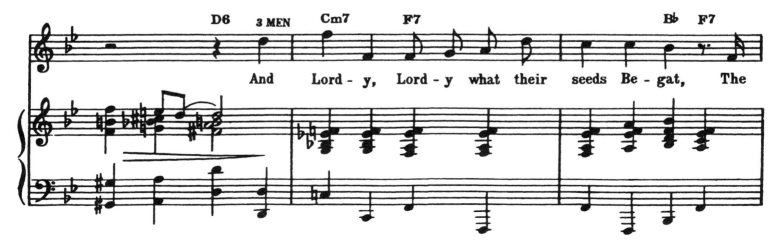

34

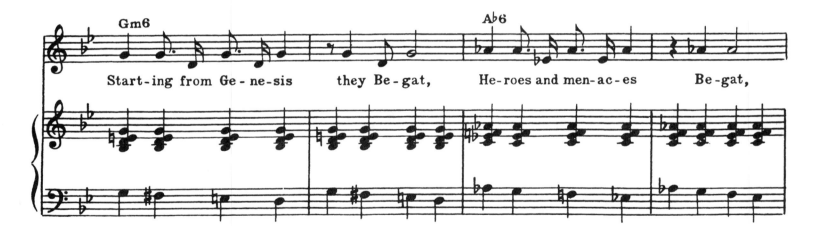

Nat-cha-ler and nat-cha-ler _____ to Be-gat, and some-times a ba-che-lor he Be-gat. It

did-n't mat-ter which-a-ways_ they Be-gat, Sons of ha-bi-tu-es Be-gat. So

bless them all _____ who go to bat, _____ And

heed the call _____ of the Be-gat. _____

BROTHER, CAN YOU SPARE A DIME?

Lyric by E.Y. "YIP" HARBURG
Music by JAY GORNEY

They used to tell me I was build-ing a dream,— And so I fol-lowed the mob

When there was earth to plough or guns to bear— I was

al-ways there— right there on the job. They used to tell me I was

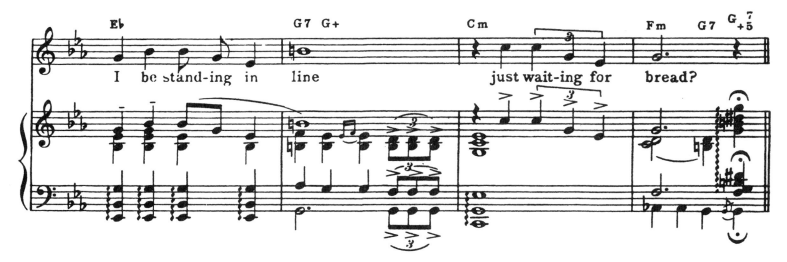

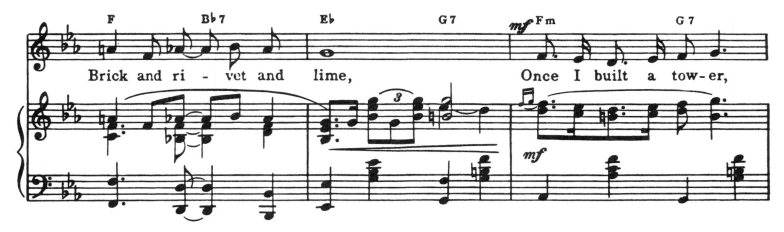

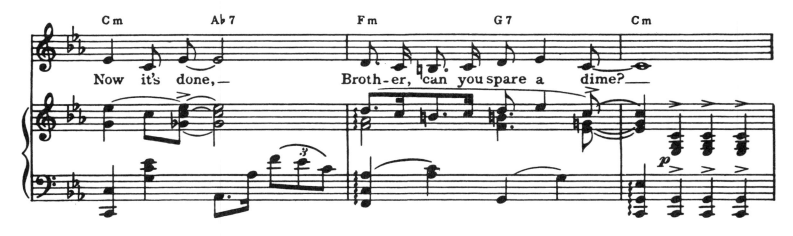

dum. Half a mil-lion boots went slog-gin' thru Hell,

I was the kid_with the drum._ Say don't you re-mem-ber, they

called me Al_ It was Al_ all the time Say, don't you re-mem-ber

I'm your Pal!_ Bud-dy, can you spare a dime?_

DOWN WITH LOVE

from the Musical Production HOORAY FOR WHAT!

Lyric by E.Y. "YIP" HARBURG
Music by HAROLD ARLEN

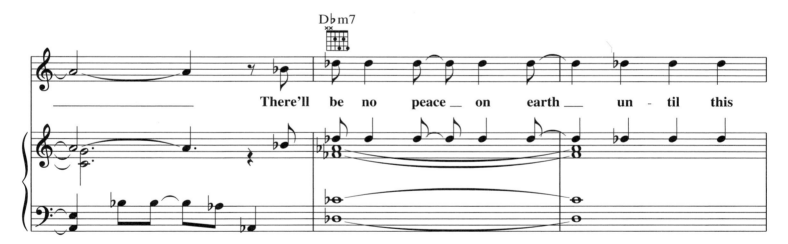

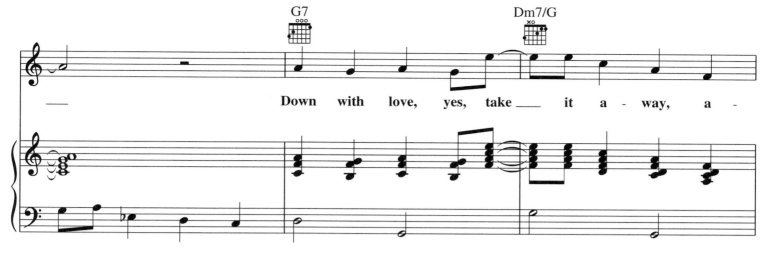

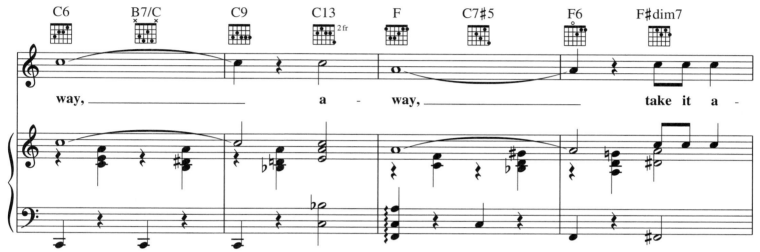

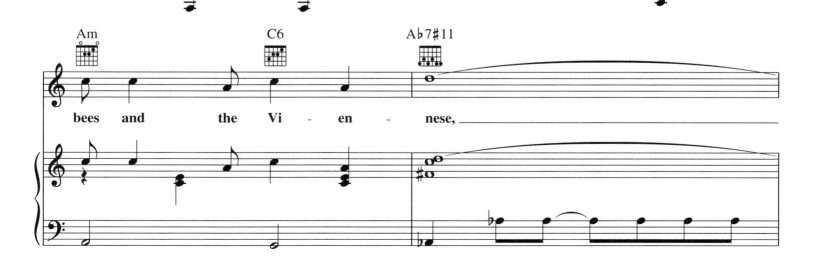

THE EAGLE AND ME
from BLOOMER GIRL

Lyric by E.Y. "YIP" HARBURG
Music by HAROLD ARLEN

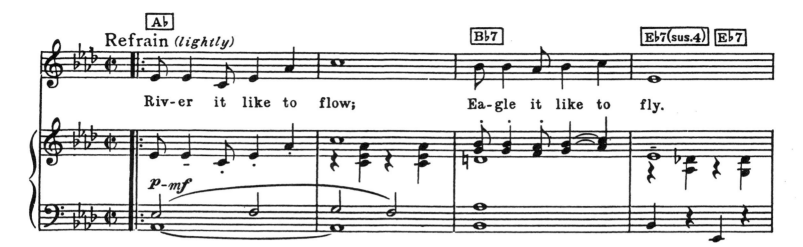

Refrain (lightly)

River it like to flow; Ea-gle it like to fly.

Ea-gle it like to feel its wings a-gainst the sky.

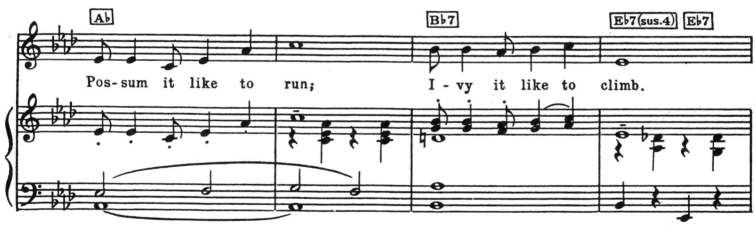

Pos-sum it like to run; I-vy it like to climb.

Bird in the tree and bum-ble bee want free-dom in au-

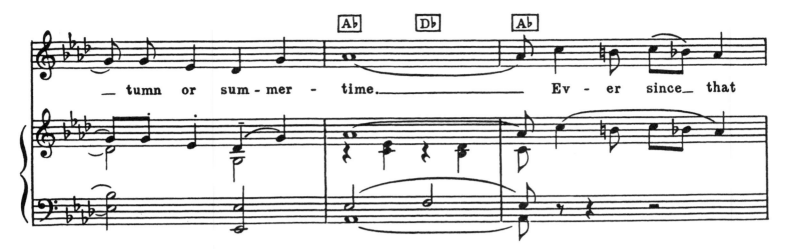

_tumn or sum-mer-time._____ Ev-er since_ that

day _____ When the world was an on-ion _____ 'Twas

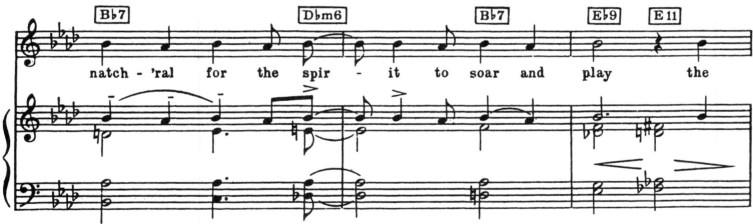

natch-'ral for the spir-it to soar and play the

way the Lawd'a-want-ed it. Free as the sun is free.

That's how it's got-ta be _____ What - ev-er is right for bum-ble bee and

riv - er, and ea - gle, is right for me. _____ We got-ta be

free _____ The ea - gle and me. _____

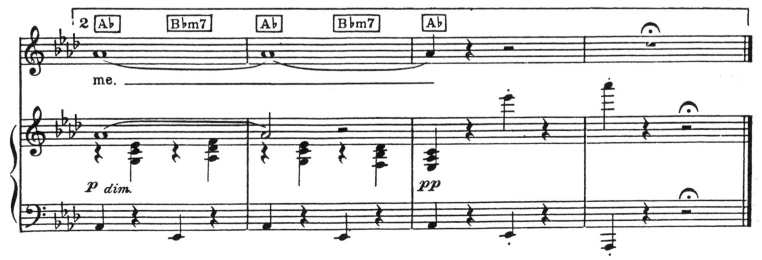

me. _____

FREE AND EQUAL BLUES

Lyric by E.Y. "YIP" HARBURG
Music by EARL ROBINSON

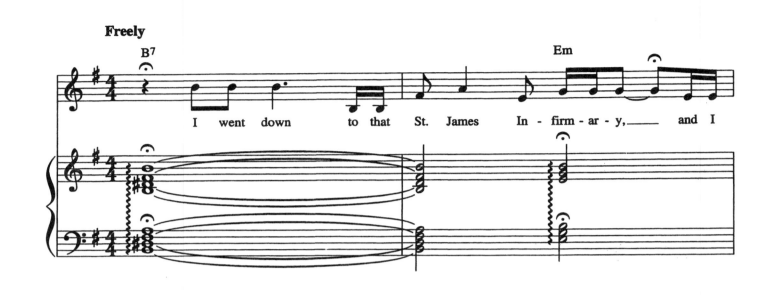

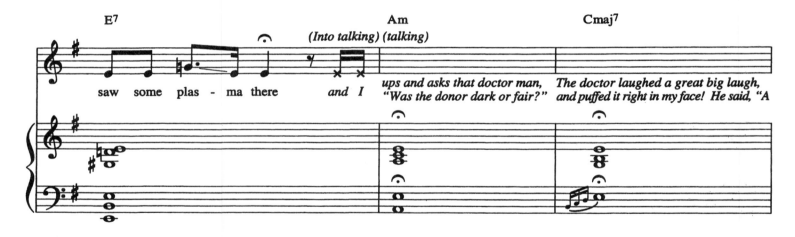

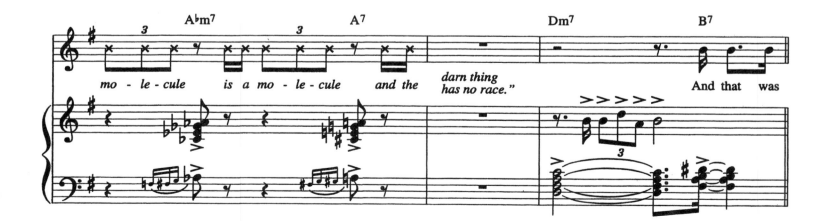

Swing tempo (♪♪ = ♪♪)
Chorus:

news,   yes that____ was   news.____   That was ver - y, ver - y, ver - y spe - cial

news.____   'Cause ev - er since that day I've got those Free and E - qual

Blues.

You mean you heard that Doc de - clare, the   plas - ma in that test____ tube there *could be*

white man, black man, yel - low man, red? That's what he said! The Doc put down his doctor book and gave me a very scientific look

Chorus:

He spoke out plain and clear and rational "Metabolism is international!" And that was

a tempo

news, yes, that__ was news._____ That was ver - y, ver - y, ver - y spe - cial

news._____ 'Cause ev - er since that day I've got those

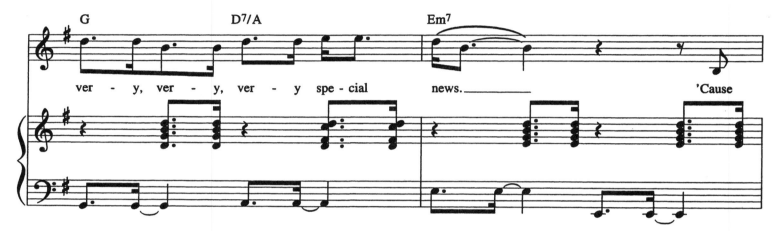

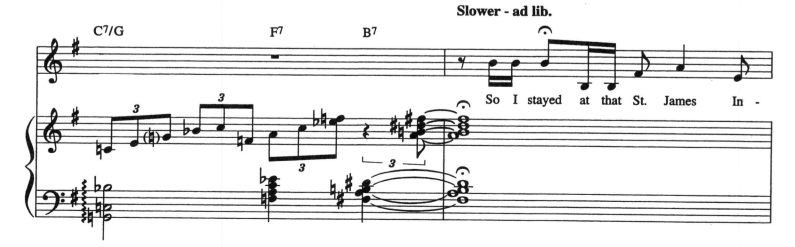

C7 A7/C# B7/D#

magnesium, a bit of sulphur, *a soupçon of Hydro-cloric acid, and you* *stir it all up.* *And what are you?*

N.C. Em B7

A walkin' drugstore.
An international
chemical cartel!

And that's the news, yes that's ___ the

rhythm

E

news. _____ So lis - ten you Af - ri - can and

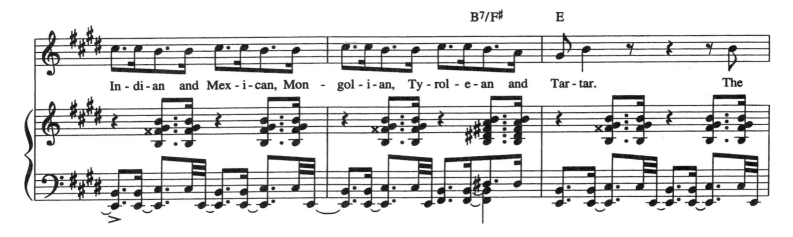

B7/F# E

In - di - an and Mex - i - can, Mon - gol - i - an, Ty - rol - e - an and Tar - tar. The

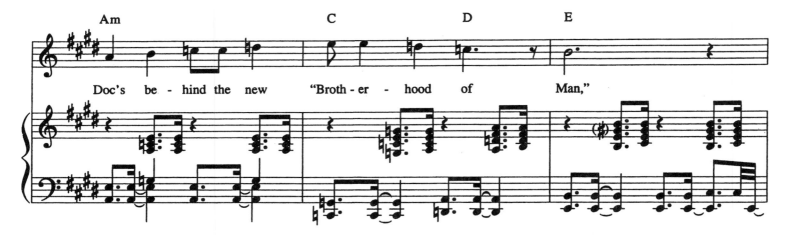

FUN TO BE FOOLED

from the Musical Production LIFE BEGINS AT 8:40

Lyric by E.Y. "YIP" HARBURG and IRA GERSHWIN
Music by HAROLD ARLEN

*Symbols for Ukulele, Tenor-Guitar and Banjo

Fools rush in to be-gin new love af-fairs,_____

But, to-night, to-night, my dear, who cares?_____

REFRAIN

Fun to be fooled,___ Fun to pre-tend;___

Fun to be-lieve___ Love is un-end-ing.

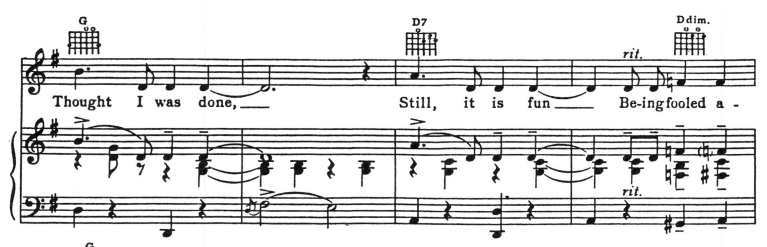

Thought I was done,____ Still, it is fun ____ Be-ing fooled a -

gain. ____ ____ Nice when you tell ____ All that you feel,____

Nice to be told ____ This is the real thing;

Fun to be kissed,____ Fun to ex - ist,____ To be fooled a - gain. ____

HAPPINESS IS A THING CALLED JOE

from the Motion Picture CABIN IN THE SKY

Words by E.Y. "YIP" HARBURG
Music by HAROLD ARLEN

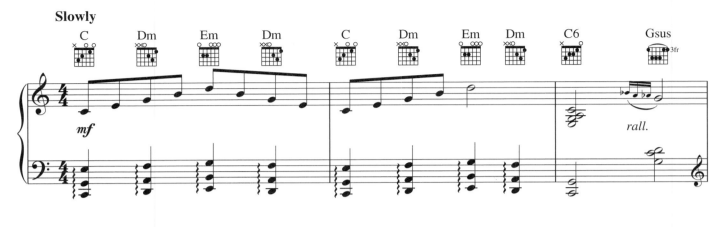

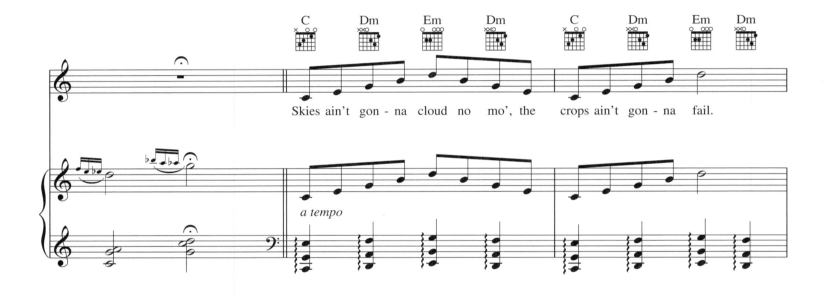

Skies ain't gon-na cloud no mo', the crops ain't gon-na fail.

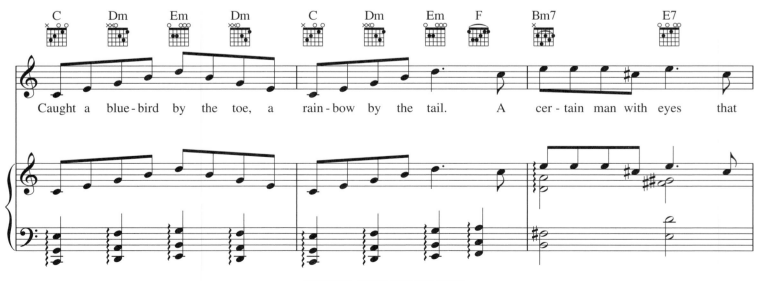

Caught a blue-bird by the toe, a rain-bow by the tail. A cer-tain man with eyes that

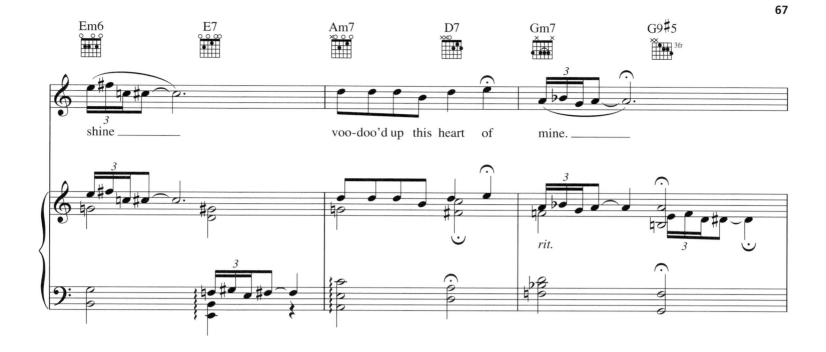

shine _____ voo-doo'd up this heart of mine. _____

It seem like

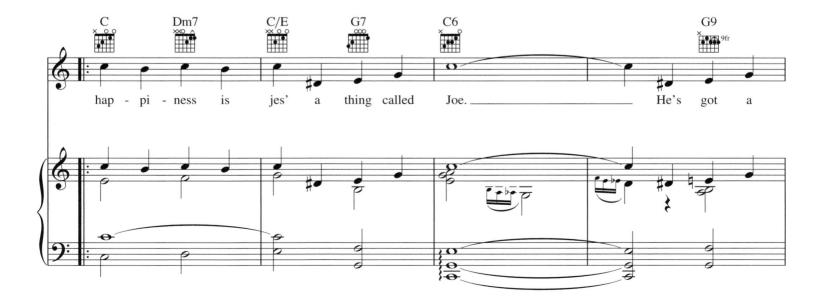

hap - pi - ness is jes' a thing called Joe. _____ He's got a

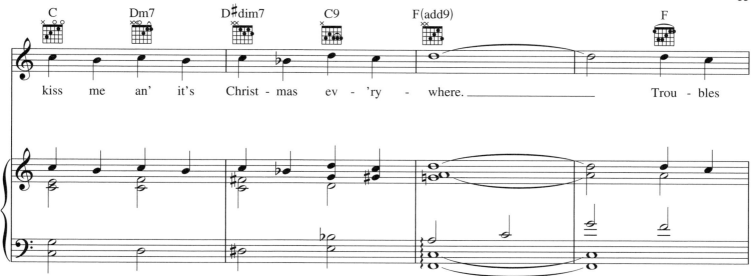

kiss me an' it's Christ - mas ev - 'ry - where._____ Trou - bles

fly a - way an' life is eas - y go._____ Does he

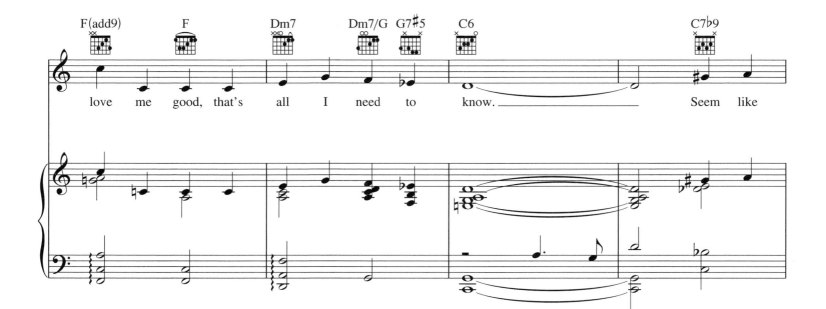

love me good, that's all I need to know._____ Seem like

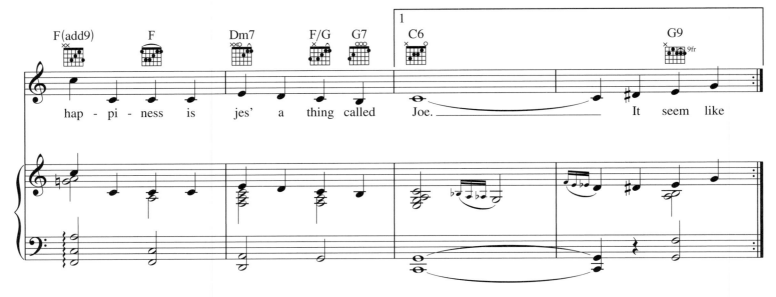

hap - pi - ness is jes' a thing called Joe. _____ It seem like

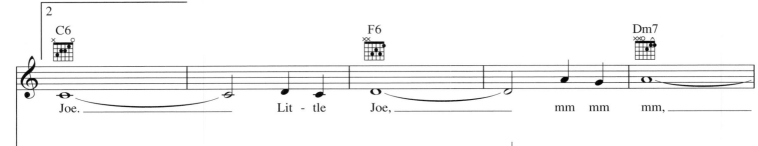

Joe. _____ Lit - tle Joe, _____ mm mm mm, _____

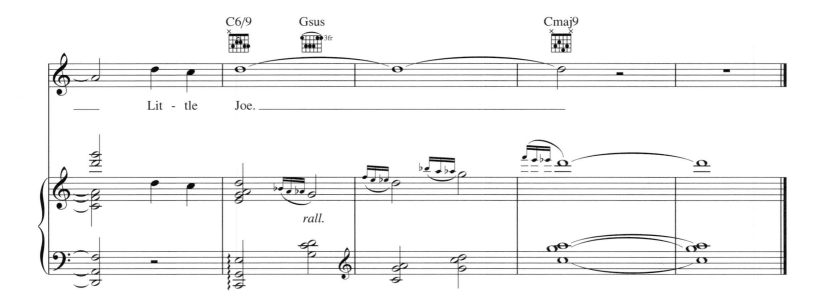

_____ Lit - tle Joe. _____

HURRY SUNDOWN

Lyric by E.Y. "YIP" HARBURG
Music by EARL ROBINSON

My seed is sown now,_____ my field is plowed.
breeze now,_____ blows clear and loud.
song now,_____ just must break through.

My flesh is bone now,_____ my back is bowed.
I'm off my knees now,_____ I'm stand-ing proud.
That brave new dawn now,_____ long o - ver - due.

So Hur-ry Sun-down,_____ be on your way_____ and hur-ry me a

sun - up from this beat-up sun___ down day. Hur - ry down sun - down,___

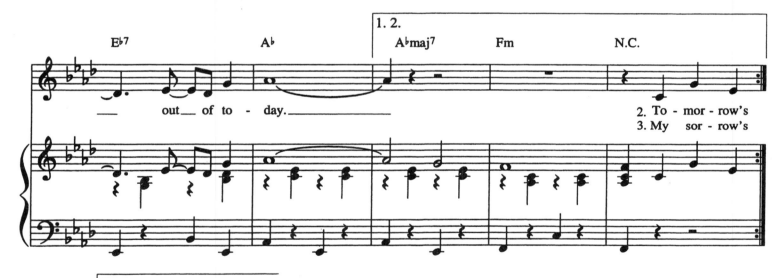

___ be on your way._____ Weave___ me to - mor - row___

___ out___ of to - day._____

2. To - mor - row's
3. My sor - row's

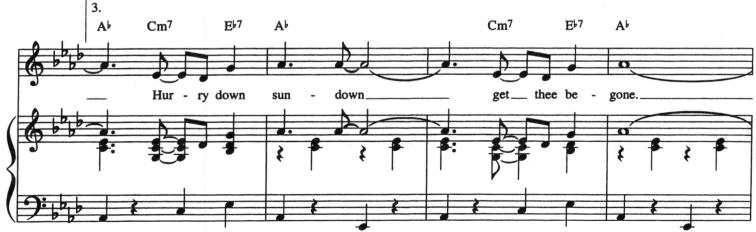

___ Hur - ry down sun - down_____ get___ thee be - gone.___

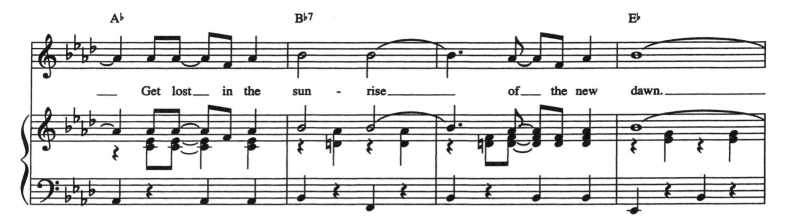

Get lost__ in the sun - rise_____ of__ the new dawn._____

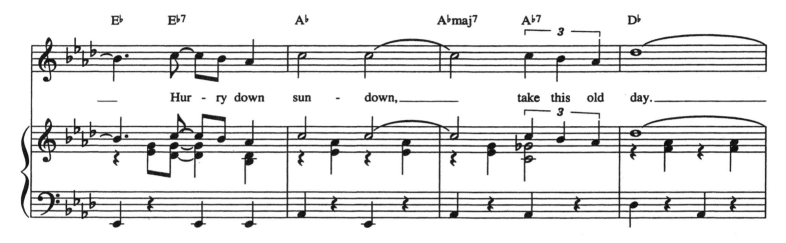

Hur - ry down sun - down,_____ take this old day._____

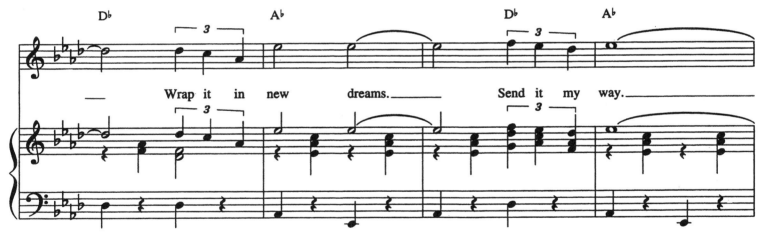

Wrap it in new dreams._____ Send it my way._____

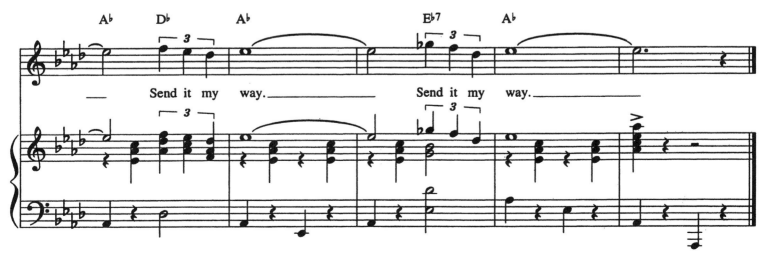

Send it my way._____ Send it my way._____

HOW ARE THINGS IN GLOCCA MORRA

from FINIAN'S RAINBOW

Words by E.Y. "YIP" HARBURG
Music by BURTON LANE

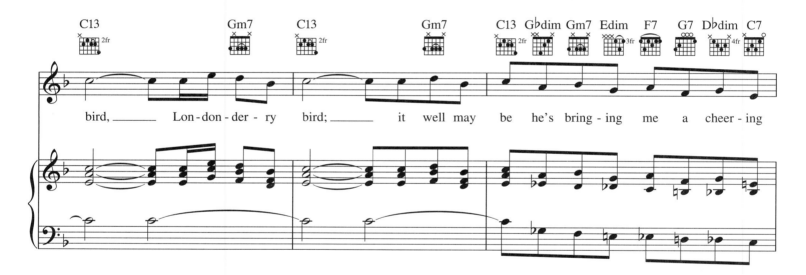

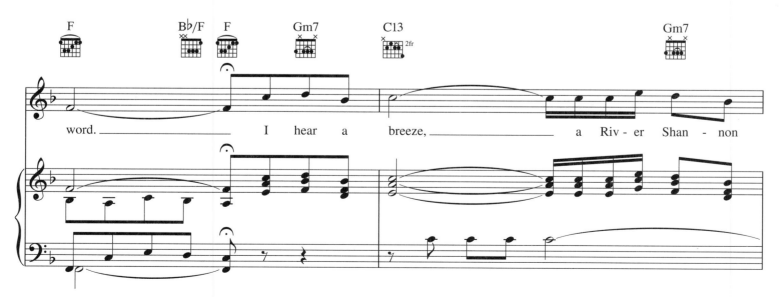

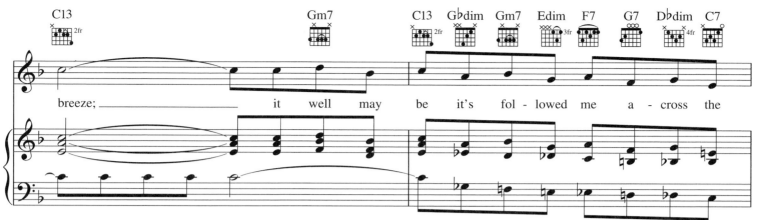

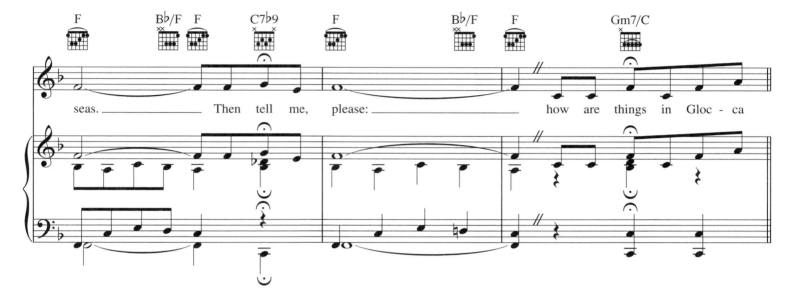

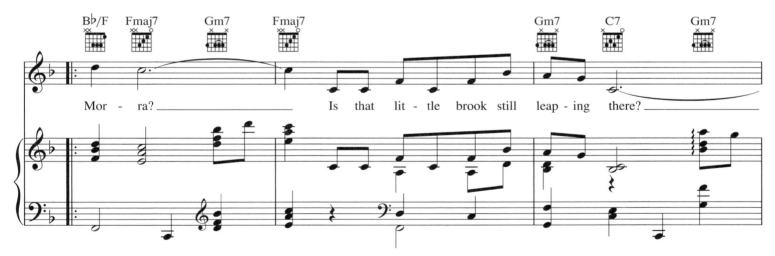

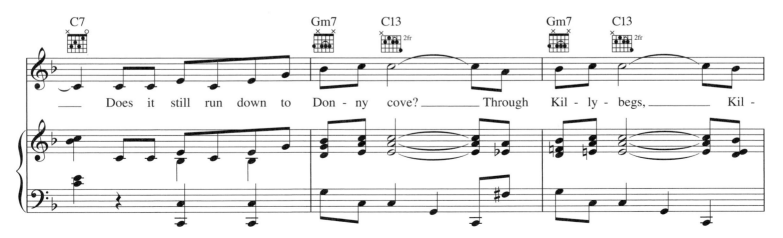

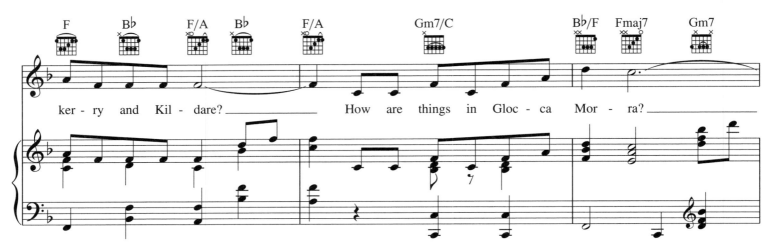

ker - ry and Kil - dare? _____ How are things in Gloc - ca Mor - ra? _____

___ Is that wil - low tree still weep - ing there? _____ Does that {lad - die / las - sie} with the

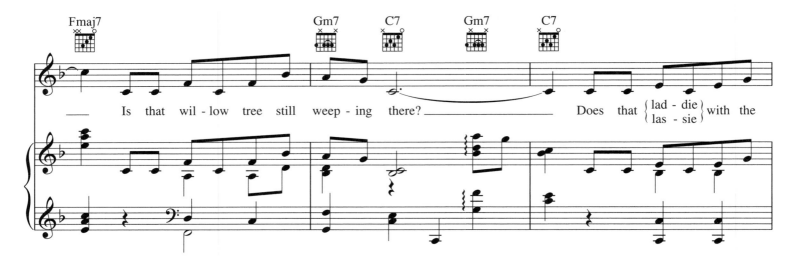

twin - klin' eye _____ come {whis - tlin' / smil - in'} by _____ and does {he / she} walk a - way, sad and

dream - y there not to see me there? _____ So I

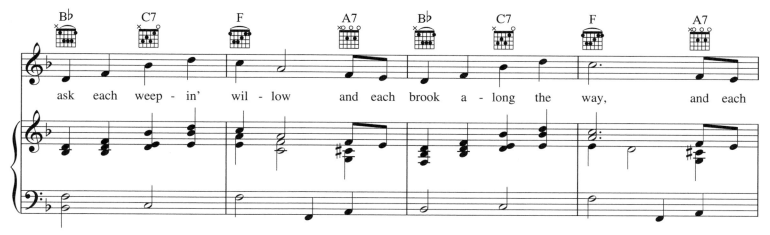

ask each weep - in' wil - low and each brook a - long the way, and each

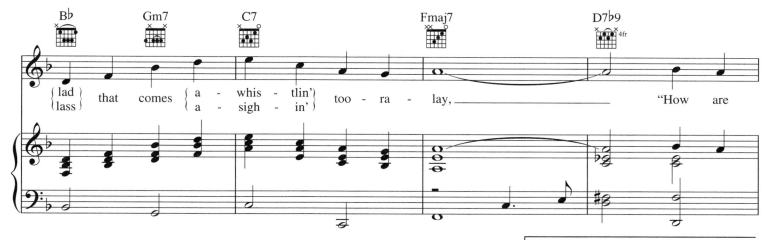

{lad} that comes {a - whis - tlin'} too - ra - lay, _____ "How are
{lass}   {a - sigh - in'}

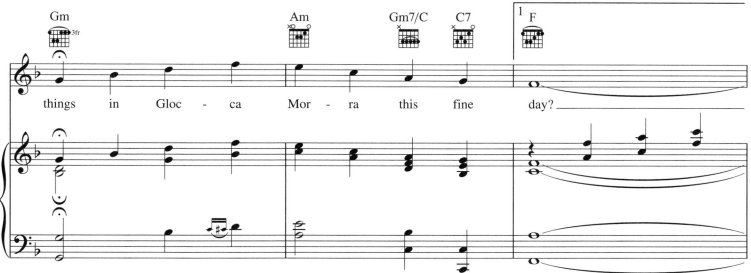

things in Gloc - ca Mor - ra this fine day? _____

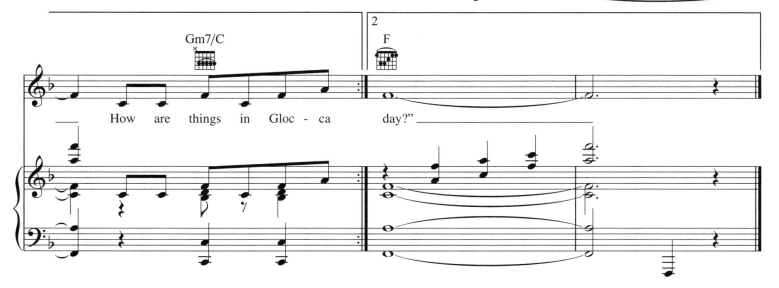

___ How are things in Gloc - ca day?" _____

I LIKE THE LIKES OF YOU

Lyric by E.Y. "YIP" HARBURG
Music by VERNON DUKE

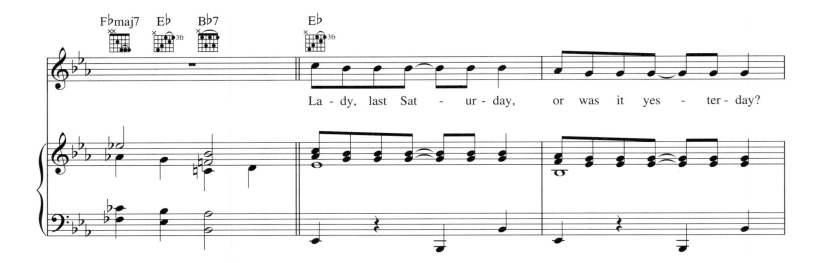

Lady, last Sat-ur-day, or was it yes-ter-day?

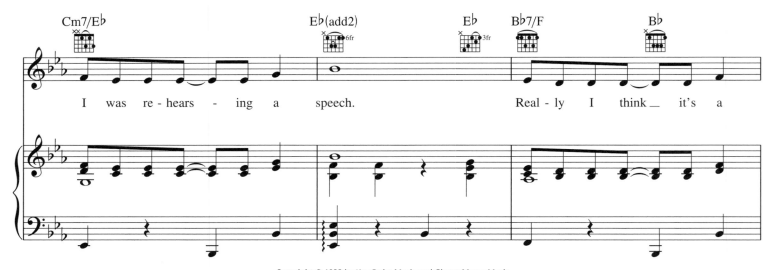

I was re-hears-ing a speech. Real-ly I think __ it's a

think they're blue, don't you? I mean I like your eyes of

blue. Oh, dear, _____ if I could on - ly say _____ what I

mean, _____ I mean if I could mean _____ what I say. _____ That is, I

mean to say _____ that I mean to say that

I like the likes of you. Your looks are pure de-

luxe. Looks like I like the likes of you. _____

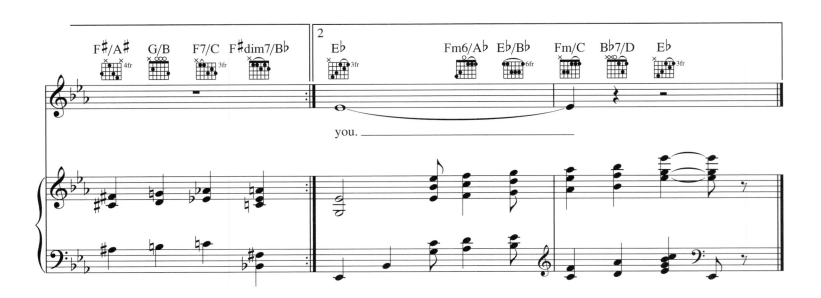

you. _____

IF I ONLY HAD A BRAIN

from THE WIZARD OF OZ

Lyric by E.Y. "YIP" HARBURG
Music by HAROLD ARLEN

Scarecrow: Said a scare-crow swing-in' on a pole ___ to a black-bird sit-tin' on a
Tin Woodman: Said a tin-man rat-tlin' his ___ gibs ___ to a straw-man sad and wea-ry-
Cowardly Lion: Said a li-on poor neu-rot-ic lion, ___ to a miss who lis-tened to him

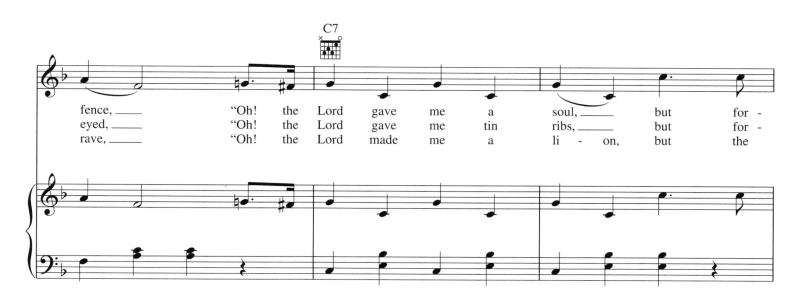

fence, ___ "Oh! the Lord gave me a soul, ___ but for-
eyed, ___ "Oh! the Lord gave me tin ribs, ___ but for-
rave, ___ "Oh! the Lord made me a li-on, but the

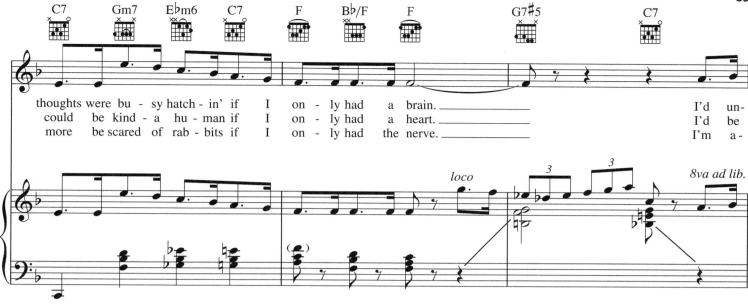

thoughts were bu - sy hatch - in' if I on - ly had a brain. _____ I'd un-
could be kind - a hu - man if I on - ly had a heart. _____ I'd be
more be scared of rab - bits if I on - ly had the nerve. _____ I'm a-

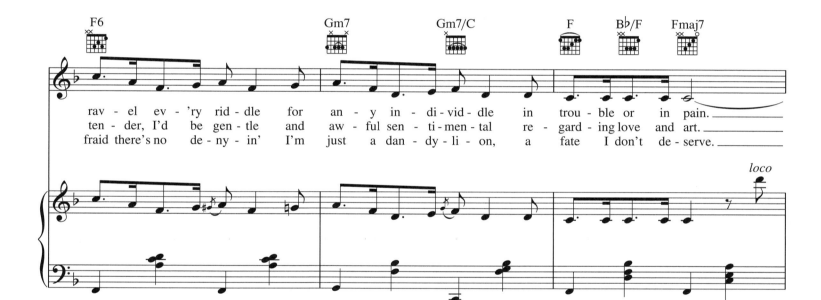

rav - el ev - 'ry rid - dle for an - y in - di - vid - dle in trou - ble or in pain. _____
ten - der, I'd be gen - tle and aw - ful sen - ti - men - tal re - gard - ing love and art. _____
fraid there's no de - ny - in' I'm just a dan - dy - li - on, a fate I don't de - serve. _____

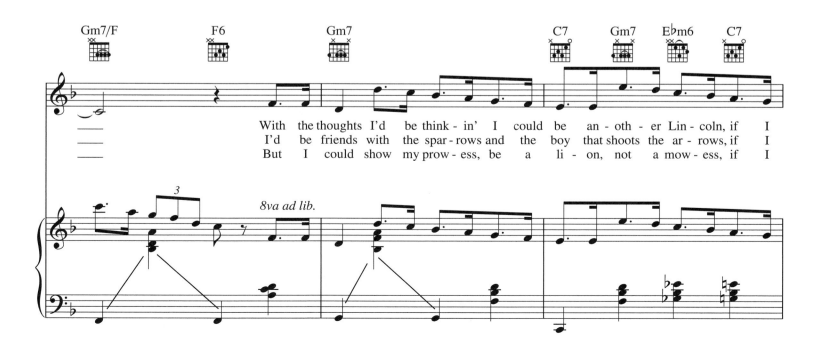

With the thoughts I'd be think - in' I could be an - oth - er Lin - coln, if I
I'd be friends with the spar - rows and the boy that shoots the ar - rows, if I
But I could show my prow - ess, be a li - on, not a mow - ess, if I

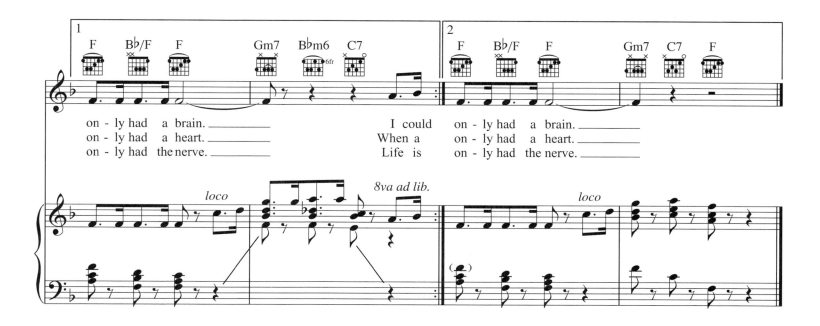

IT'S ONLY A PAPER MOON

Lyric by BILLY ROSE and E.Y. "YIP" HARBURG
Music by HAROLD ARLEN

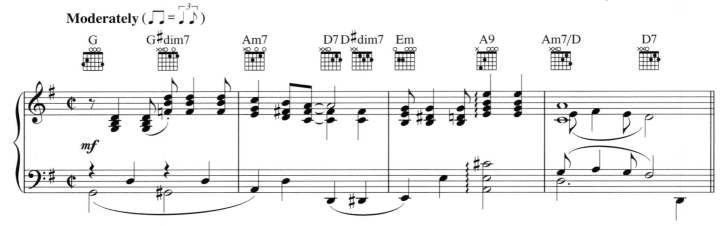

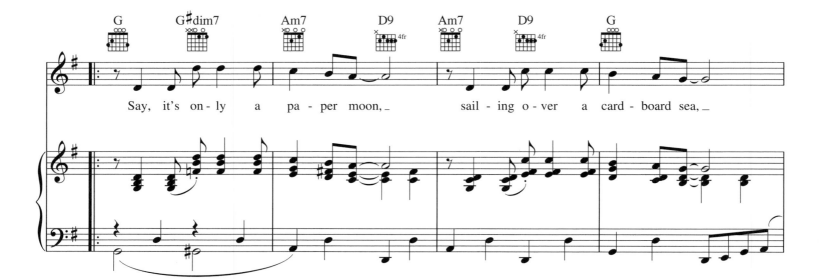

Say, it's on-ly a pa-per moon, sail-ing o-ver a card-board sea,

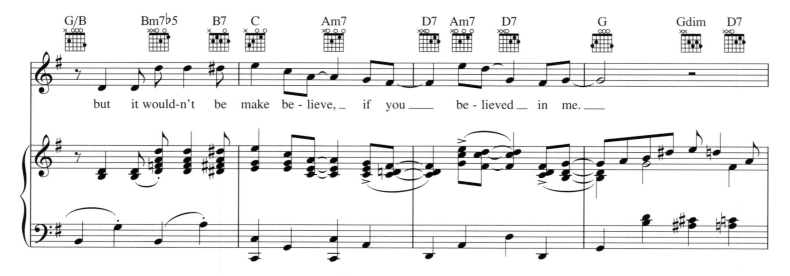

but it would-n't be make be-lieve, if you be-lieved in me.

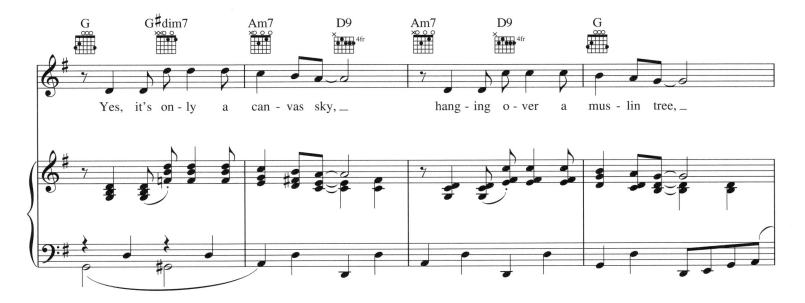

Yes, it's on-ly a can-vas sky, __ hang-ing o-ver a mus-lin tree, __

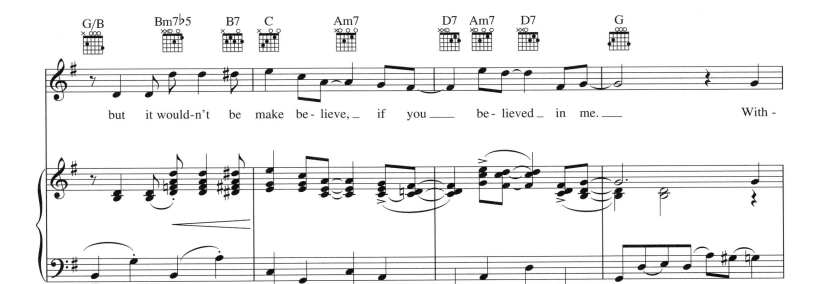

but it would-n't be make be-lieve, __ if you ___ be-lieved __ in me. ___ With-

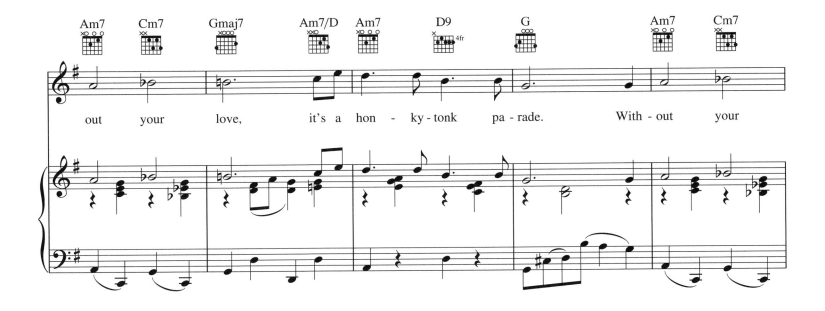

out your love, it's a hon-ky-tonk pa-rade. With-out your

LAST NIGHT
WHEN WE WERE YOUNG

Lyric by E.Y. "YIP" HARBURG
Music by HAROLD ARLEN

LET'S SEE WHAT HAPPENS

Lyric by E.Y. "YIP" HARBURG
Music by JULE STYNE

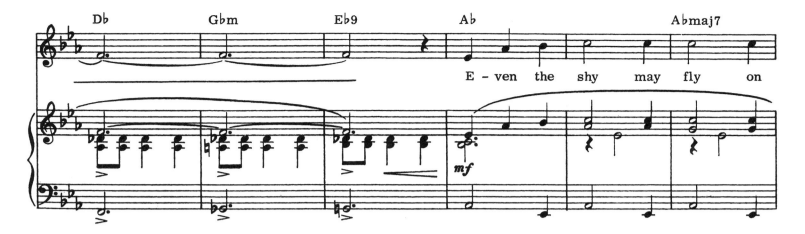

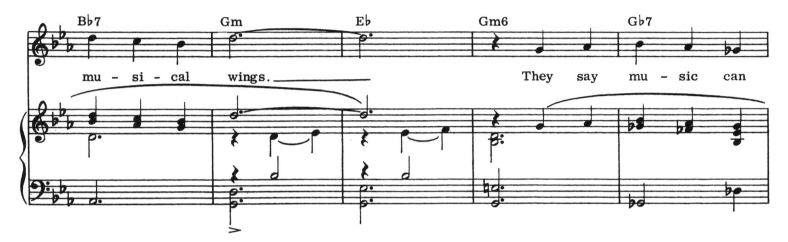

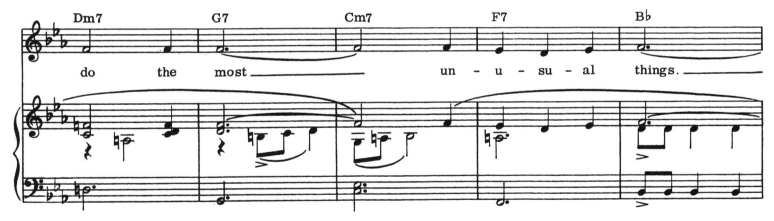

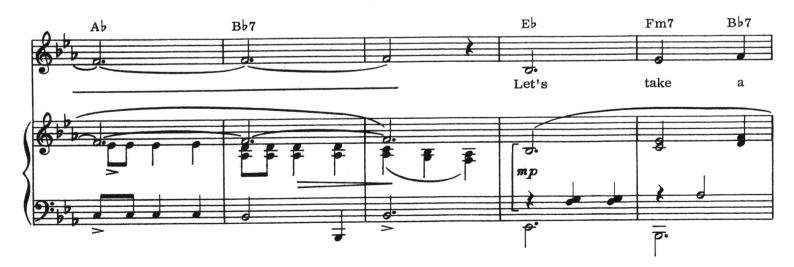

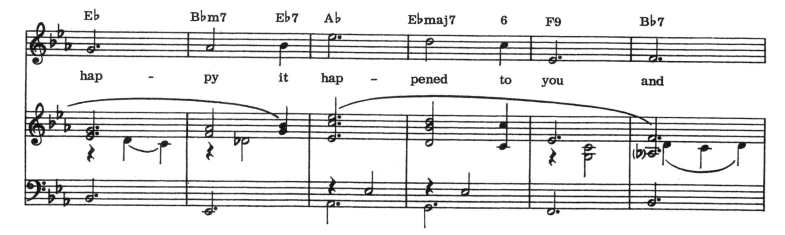

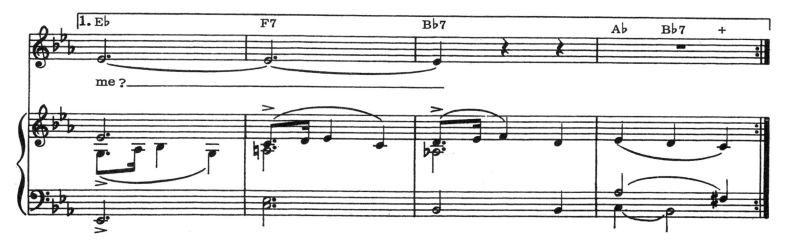

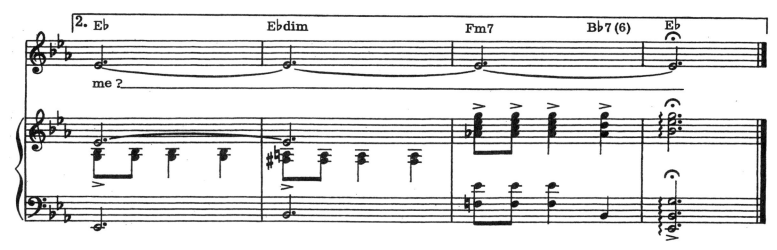

LOOK TO THE RAINBOW

from FINIAN'S RAINBOW

Words by E.Y. "Yip" HARBURG
Music by BURTON LANE

LYDIA, THE TATTOOED LADY

Lyric by E.Y. "YIP" HARBURG
Music by HAROLD ARLEN

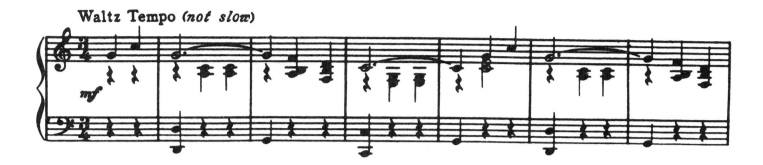

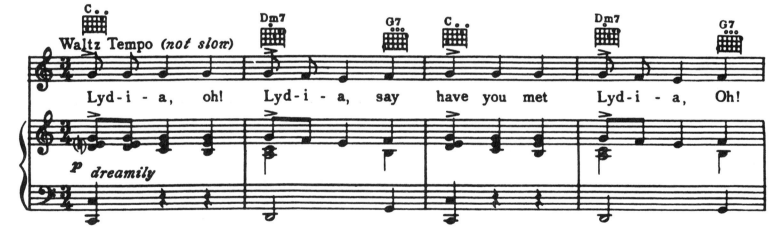

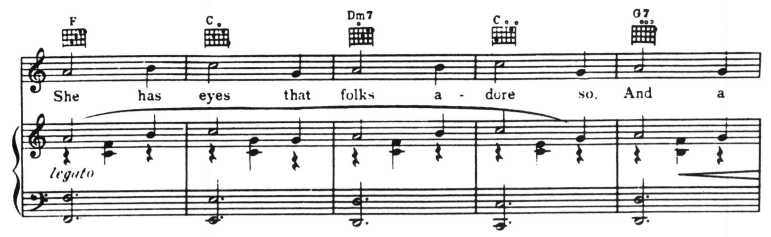

She has eyes that folks a - dore so, And a

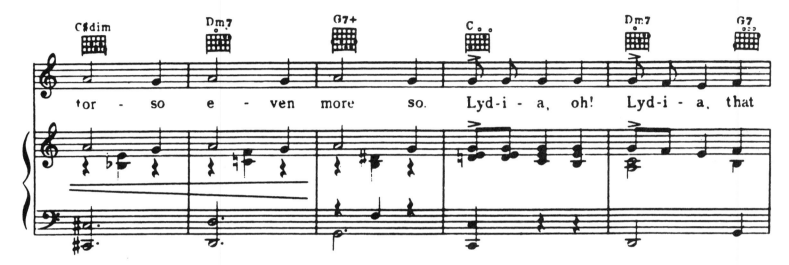

tor - so e - ven more so. Lyd-i - a, oh! Lyd-i - a, that

"En - cy - clo - pe - di - a", Oh! Lyd-i - a, the Queen of tat - too.

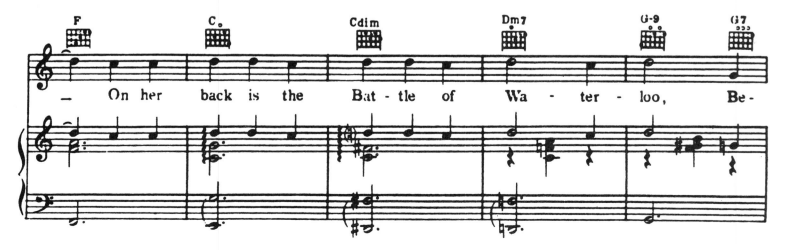

On her back is the Bat - tle of Wa - ter - loo, Be-

give you a view of the world in tat - too if you step up and tell her where

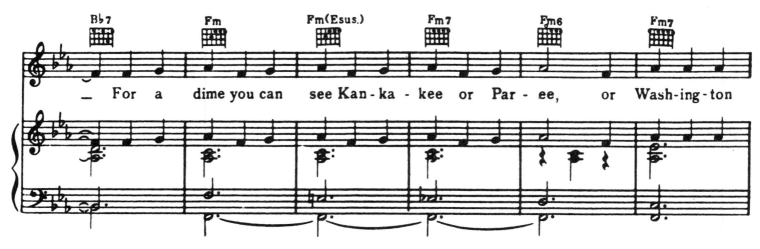

For a dime you can see Kan - ka - kee or Par - ee, or Wash - ing - ton

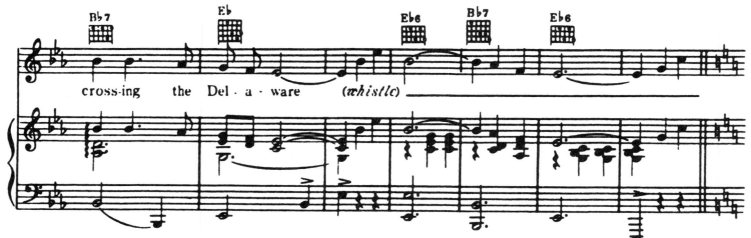

cross - ing the Del - a - ware (whistle)

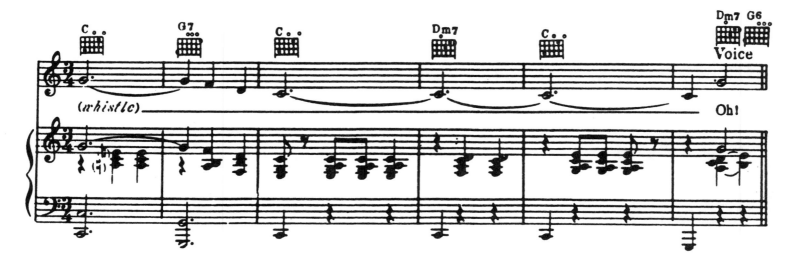

(whistle) Oh!

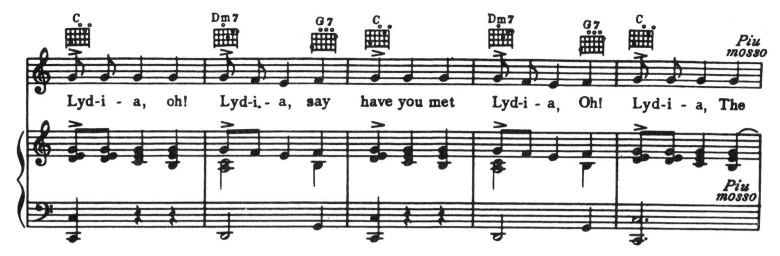

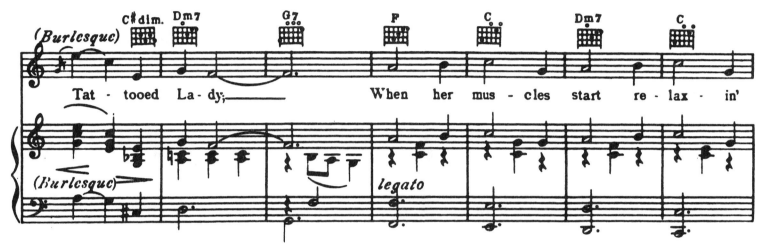

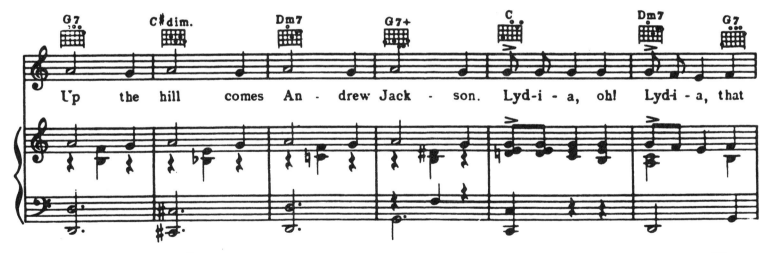

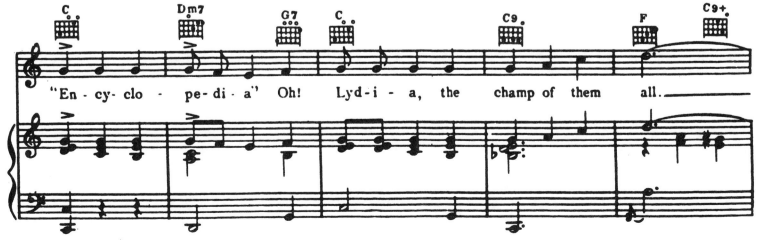

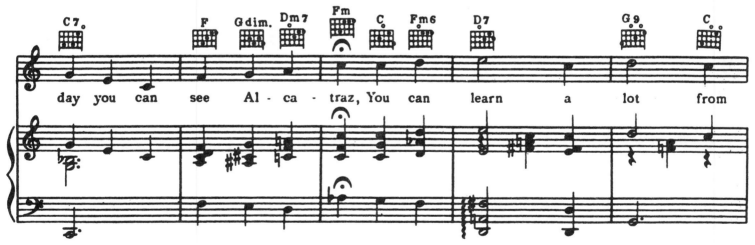

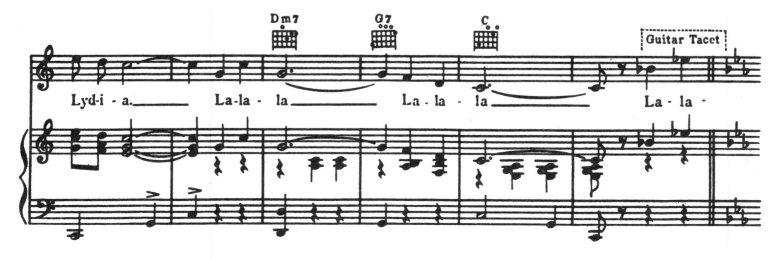

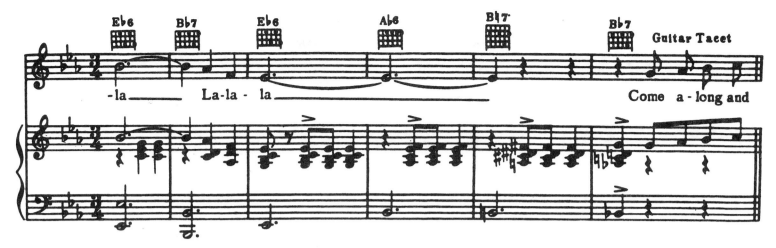

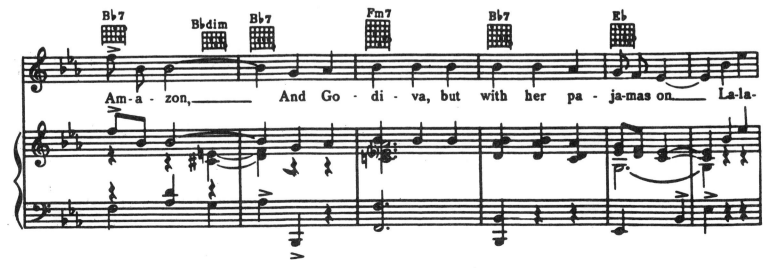

108

MUNCHKINLAND

Lyric by E.Y. "YIP" HARBURG
Music by HAROLD ARLEN

star. Kan-sas she says is the name of the star.

She brings you good news or have-n't you heard? When she fell out of

Kan-sas a mir - a-cle oc - curred. *(Spoken)* It

real-ly was no mir-a-cle, what hap-pened was just this. The wind be-gan to

switch, the house to pitch, and sud-den-ly the hing-es start-ed

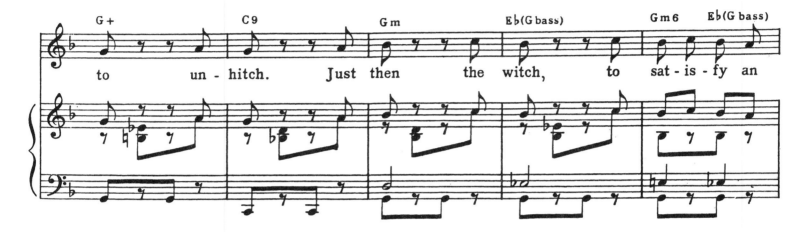

to un - hitch. Just then the witch, to sat-is-fy an

itch went fly-ing on her broom-stick thumb-ing for a hitch. And oh, what

hap-pen'd then was rich. The house be-gan to pitch, the

kitch-en took a slitch, it land-ed on the wick-ed witch in the mid-dle of a

ditch. Which _____ was not a health-y sit - u - a-tion for a wick-ed

1. witch. The 2. witch who _____ be-gan to twitch and was re - duced to just a

stitch of what was once the wick - ed witch.

rit. *f* *a tempo*

NAPOLEON
from JAMAICA

Lyric by E.Y. "YIP" HARBURG
Music by HAROLD ARLEN

Moderate strong blues

Na - po - le - on's a pas - try.
Du Bar - ry is a lip - stick.

Bis - marck is a her - ring.
Pom - pa - dour's a hair - do.

Na - po - le - on's a pas - try. ____

Bet-ter get your jug of wine and loaf of love be-fore that fi - nal bow. ____

G7#5   C9   C7♭9   F

rit.

a tempo

NECESSITY

Lyric by E.Y. "YIP" HARBURG
Music by BURTON LANE

Recitative (very slowly)

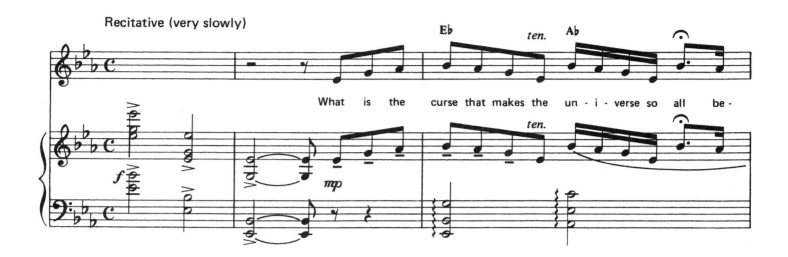

What is the curse that makes the u-i-verse so all be-

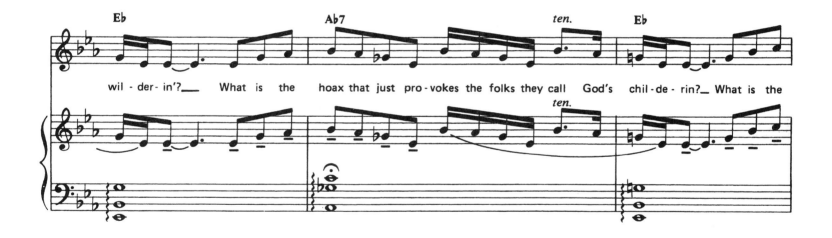

wil-der-in'?___ What is the hoax that just pro-vokes the folks they call God's chil-de-rin?__ What is the

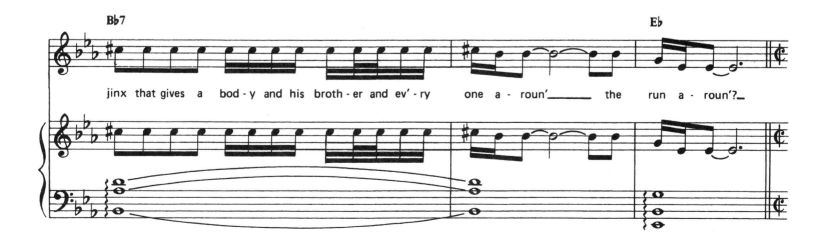

jinx that gives a bod-y and his broth-er and ev'-ry one a-roun'_____ the run a-roun'?__

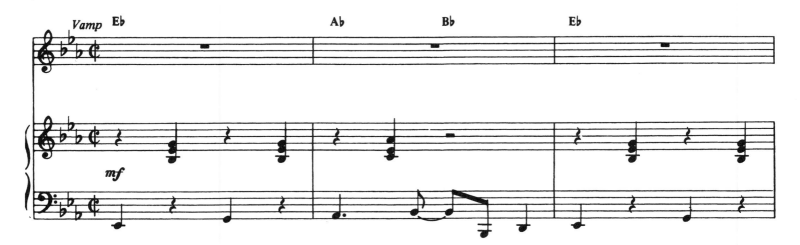

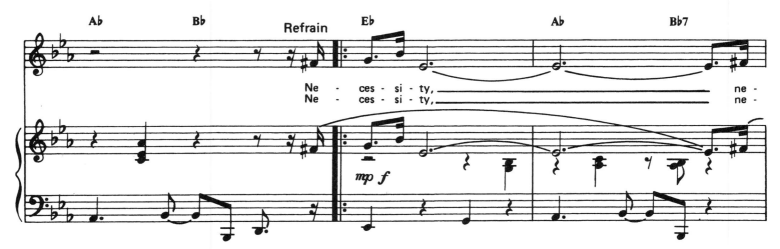

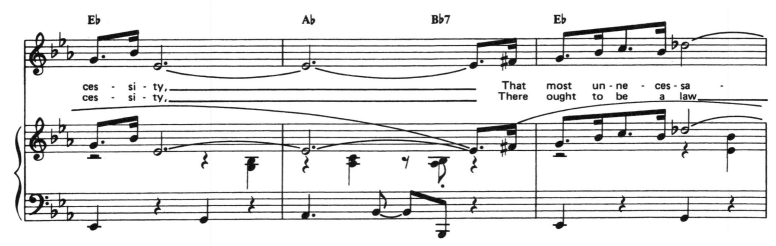

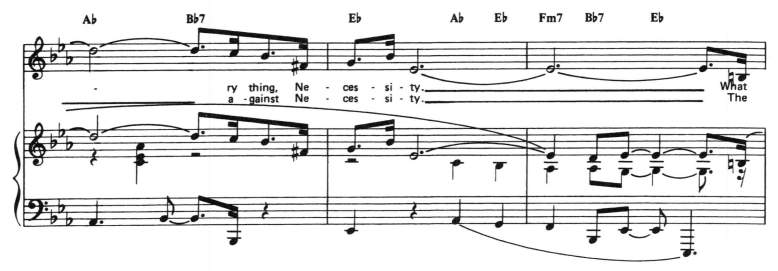

throws the mon - key wrench _____ in _____ a fel - low's good in - ten -
jail would nev - er been _____ there, _____ Ex - cept for folks who sin _____

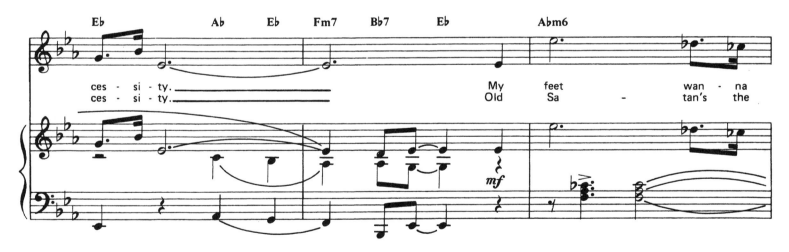

- tion, That nas - ty old in - ven - tion, _____ Ne -
there. _____ Well, how did I get in _____ there, _____ Ne -

ces - si - ty. _____ My feet wan - na
ces - si - ty. _____ Old Sa - tan's the

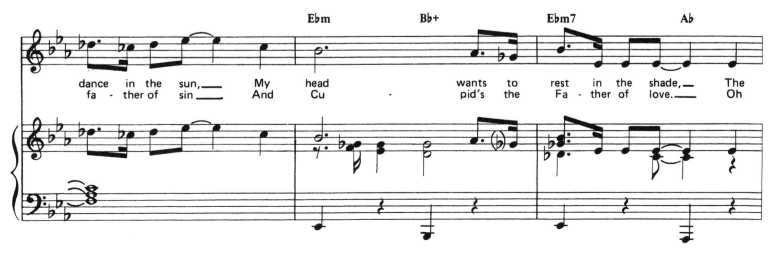

dance in the sun, _____ My head wants to rest in the shade, _____ The
fa - ther of sin _____ And Cu - pid's the Fa - ther of love. _____ Oh

Lord says "go out and have fun," ___ but the
hell is the Fa - ther of gin. ___ Ah, but the land - lord says "your
no one knows "your

rent ain't paid." ___ Ne - ces - si - ty,
Fa - ther of ___ Ne - ces - si - ty, *(You mean he's a ____?)(That's right, Brother)* It's
Ne -

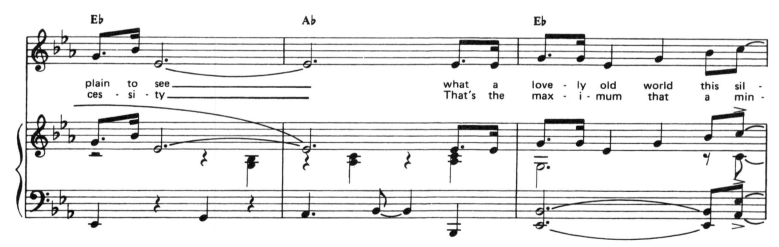

plain to see ___ what a love - ly old world this sil -
ces - si - ty ___ That's the max - i - mum that a min -

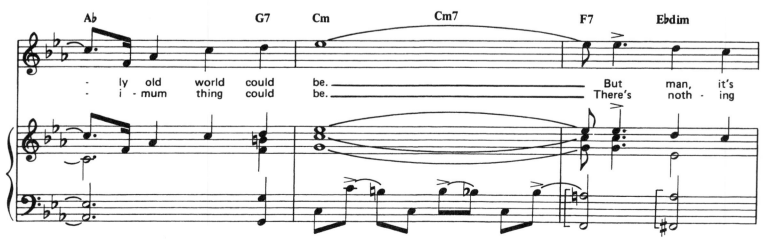

- ly old world could be. ___ But man, it's
- i - mum thing could be. ___ There's noth - ing

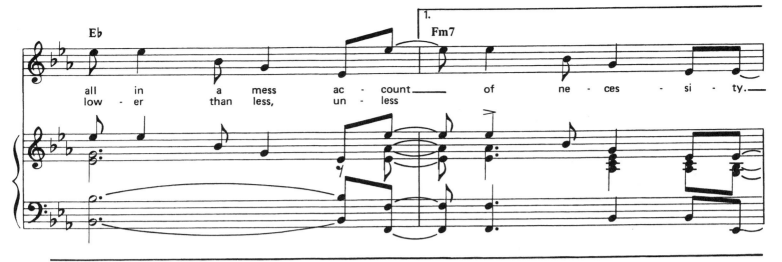

all in a mess, ac - count____ of ne - ces - si - ty.____
low - er than less, un - less

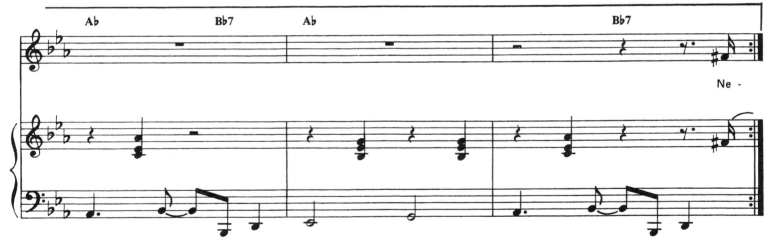

Ne -

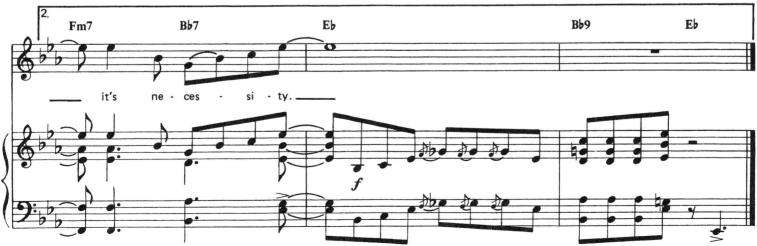

____ it's ne - ces - si - ty.____

OLD DEVIL MOON

from FINIAN'S RAINBOW

Words by E.Y. "YIP" HARBURG
Music by BURTON LANE

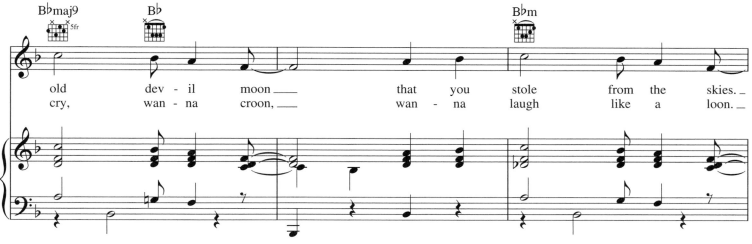

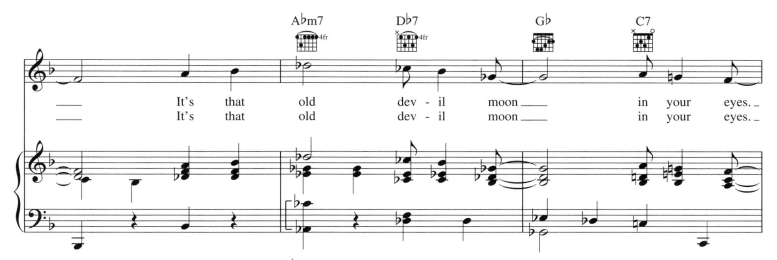

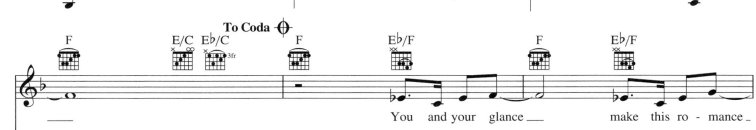

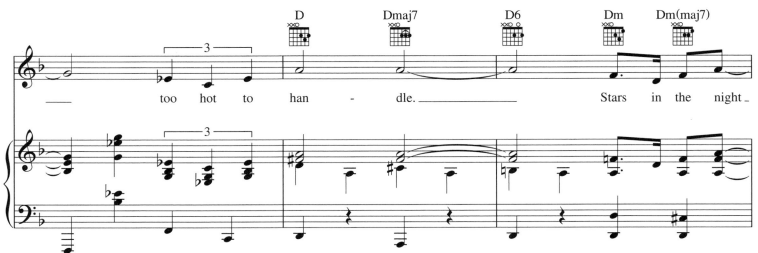

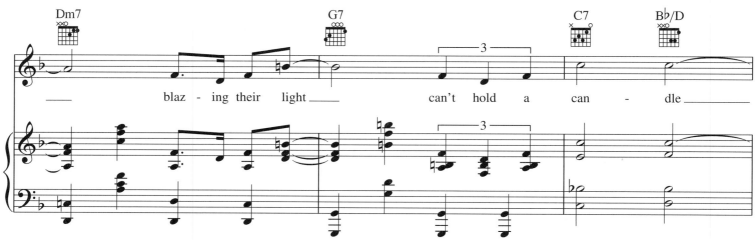

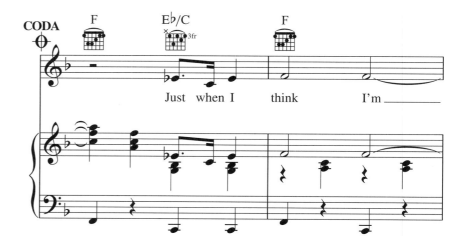

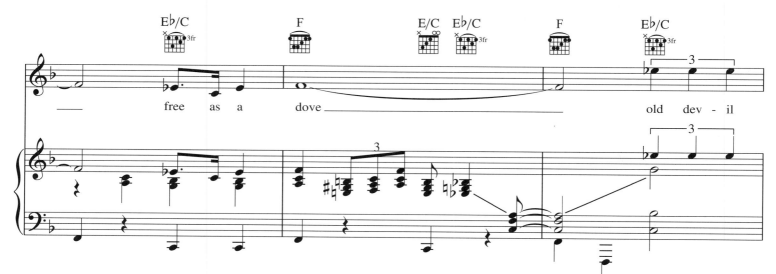

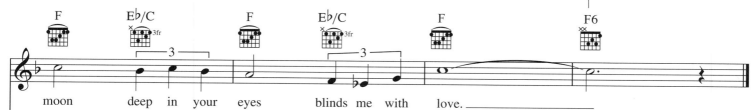

OVER THE RAINBOW
from THE WIZARD OF OZ

Lyric by E.Y. "YIP" HARBURG
Music by HAROLD ARLEN

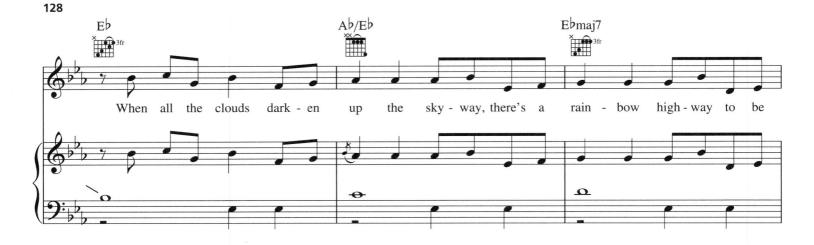

When all the clouds dark-en up the sky-way, there's a rain-bow high-way to be

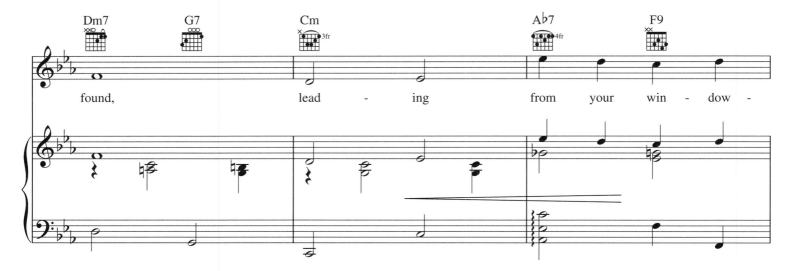

found, lead - ing from your win - dow -

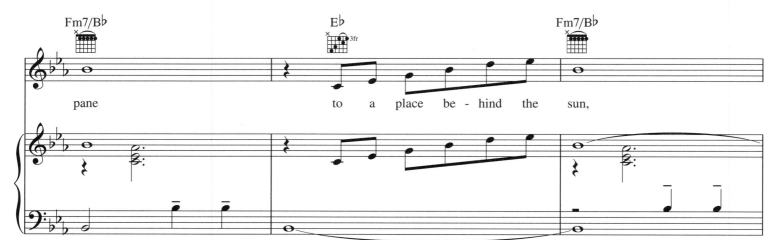

pane to a place be-hind the sun,

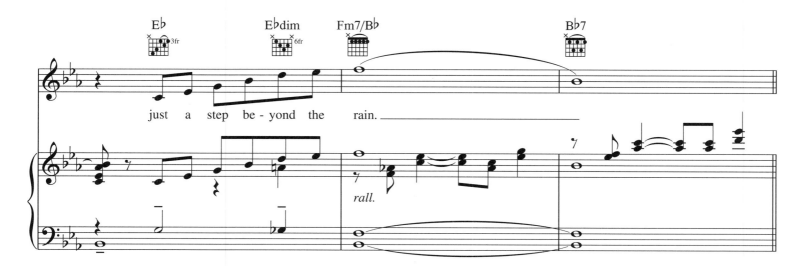

just a step be-yond the rain.

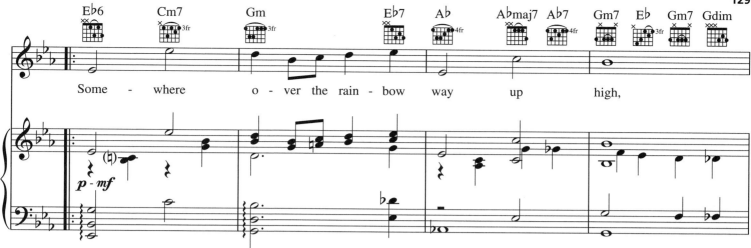

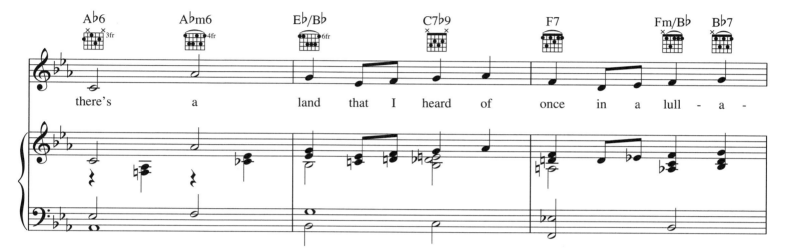

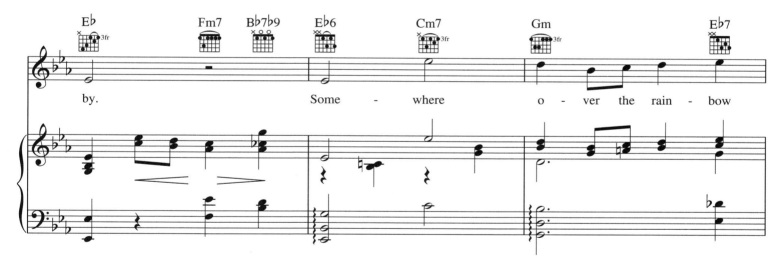

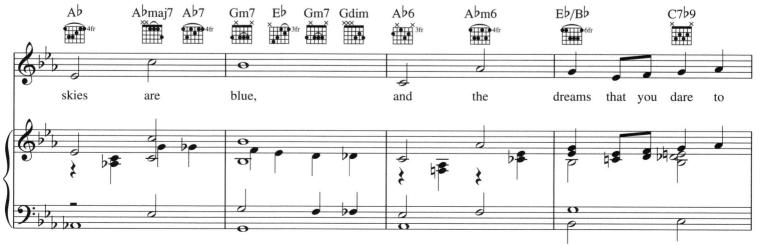

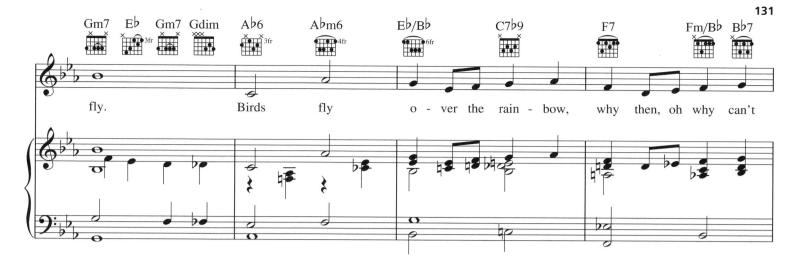

fly. Birds fly o - ver the rain - bow, why then, oh why can't

I? I?

rall.

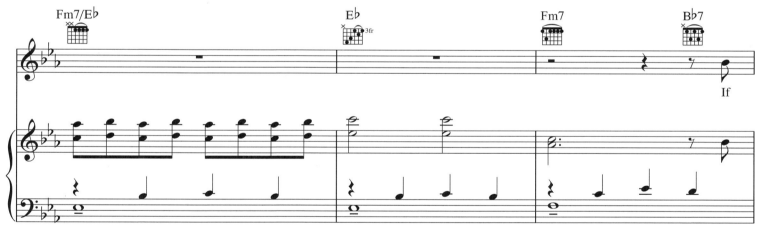

If

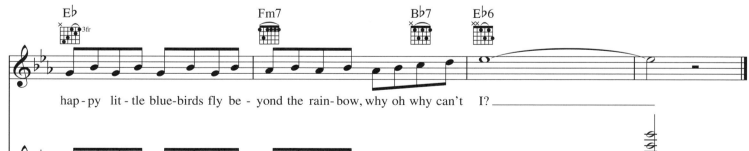

hap - py lit - tle blue-birds fly be - yond the rain-bow, why oh why can't I? _____

rit. **pp** *L.H.* *ten.*

POOR YOU

Lyric by E.Y. "YIP" HARBURG
Music by HAROLD ARLEN

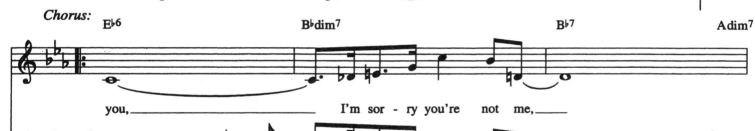

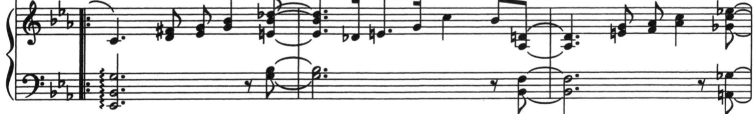

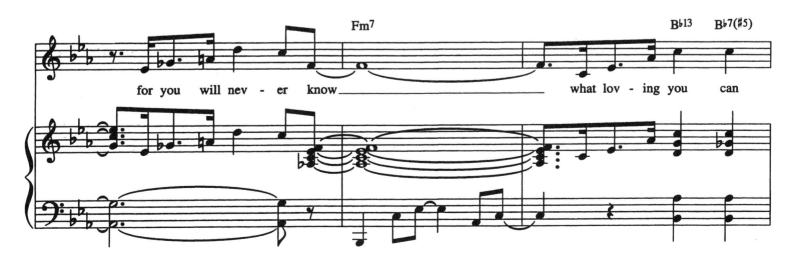

RIGHT AS THE RAIN

from BLOOMER GIRL

Lyric by E.Y. "YIP" HARBURG
Music by HAROLD ARLEN

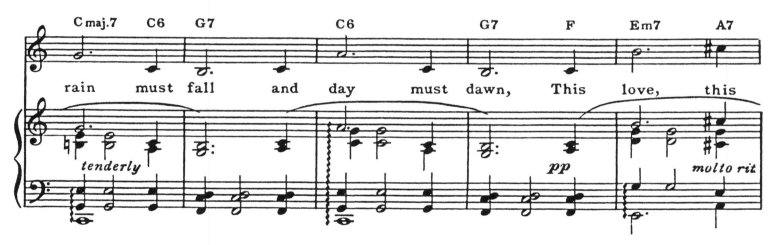

SOMETHING SORT OF GRANDISH
from FINIAN'S RAINBOW

Lyric by E.Y. "YIP" HARBURG
Music by BURTON LANE

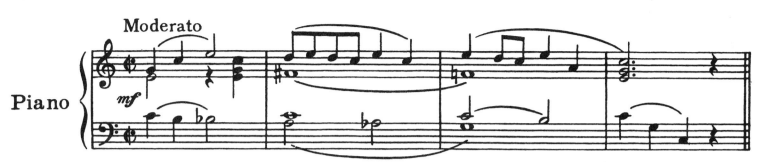

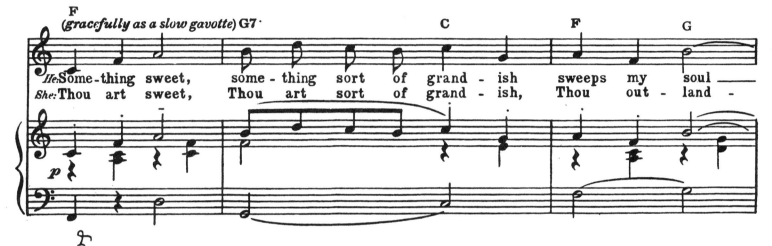

He: Some-thing sweet, some-thing sort of grand-ish sweeps my soul ___
She: Thou art sweet, Thou art sort of grand-ish, Thou out-land-

When thou art near, my heart feels ___ so sug-ar can-dish
-ish ca-va-lier. From now on, ___ we're hand in hand-ish

My head feels ___ so gin-ger beer, Some-thing so dare-ish ___
Ro-me-o ___ He: And Guin-e-vere Thou'rt so a-dor-ish ___

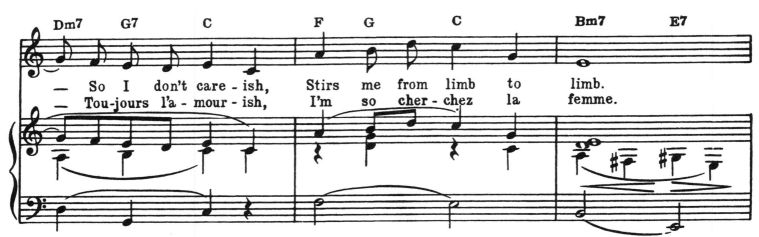

So I don't care-ish, Stirs me from limb to limb.
Tou-jours l'a-mour-ish, I'm so cher-chez la femme.

It's so ter-ri-fish, mag-ni-fish, de-lish, To have such an a-mor-ish
She: Why should I van-quish re-lin-quish, re-sish, When I sim-ply re-lish this

glam-or-ish dish. We could be oh, so bride and groom-ish
swell-ish con-dish. *He:* I might be man-ish-ish or mouse-ish,

Skies could be _____ so blue-ish blue. Life could be _____
I might be, _____ a fowl or fish, But with thee _____

THE SAME BOAT, BROTHER

Lyric by E.Y. "YIP" HARBURG
Music by EARL ROBINSON

Tempo I

took some time for the crew to learn what's bad for the bow ain't good for the stern.

If a hatch takes fire in Chin-a Bay, Pearl

D.S. 𝄋 al Coda

Har-bor's decks gon-na blaze a - way. 'Cause it's the

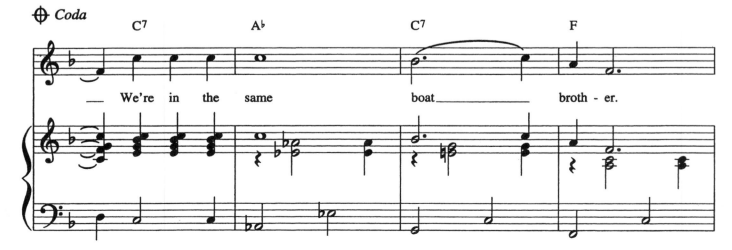

Coda

We're in the same boat broth - er.

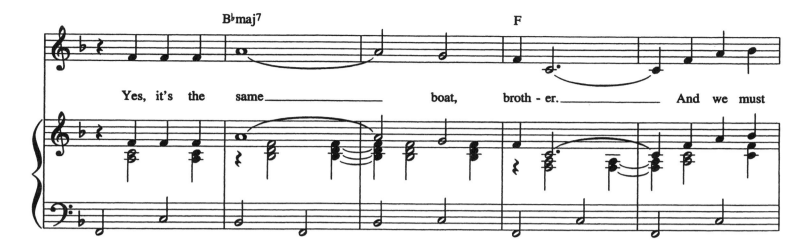

Yes, it's the same_____ boat, broth-er._____ And we must

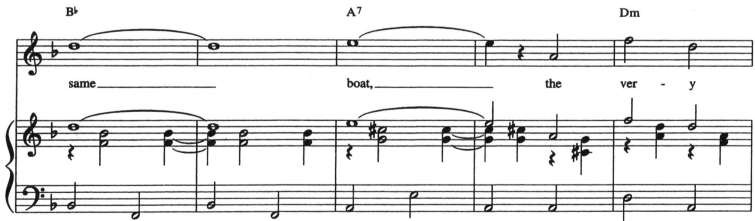

live with each oth-er_____ in the

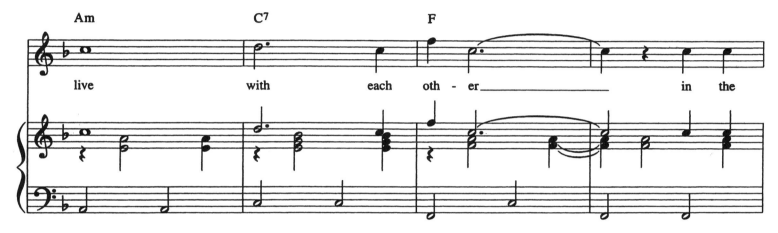

same_____ boat,_____ the ver-y

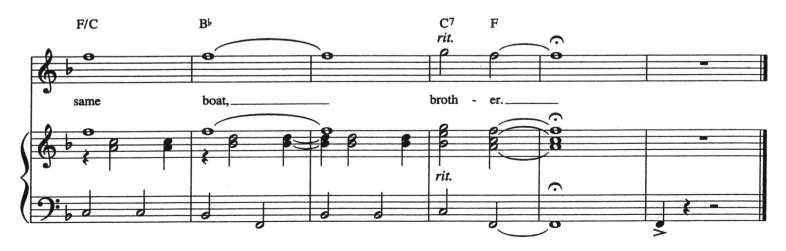

same_____ boat,_____ broth-er._____

THE SILENT SPRING

Lyric by E.Y. "YIP" HARBURG
Music by HAROLD ARLEN

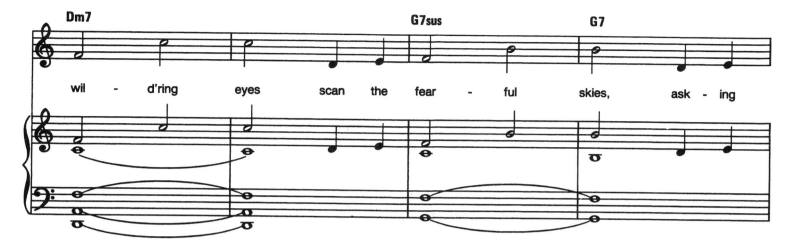

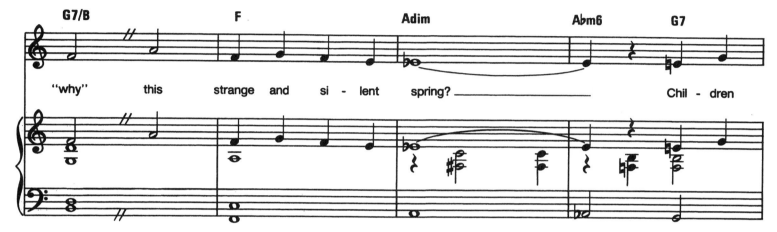

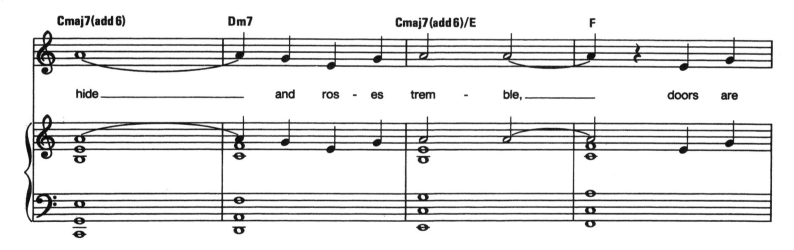

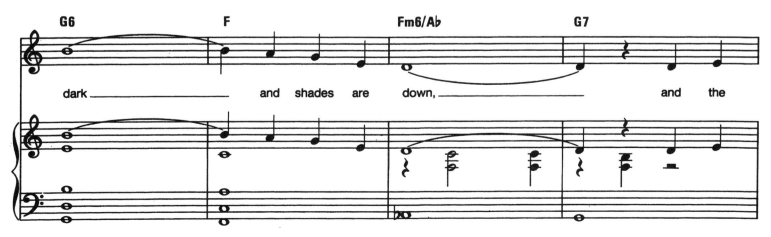

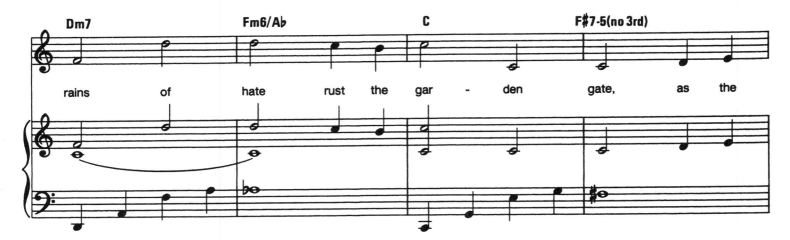

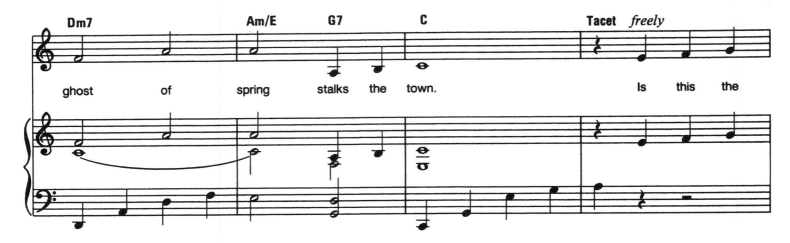

THEN I'LL BE TIRED OF YOU

Lyric by E.Y. "YIP" HARBURG
Music by ARTHUR SCHWARTZ

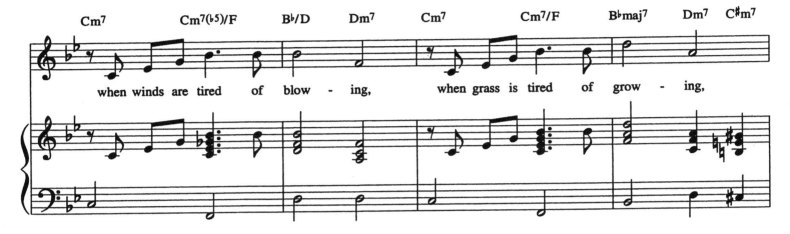

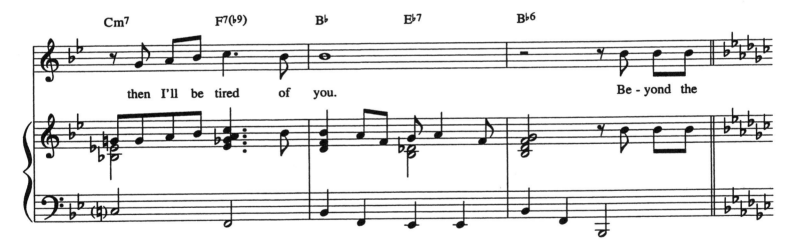

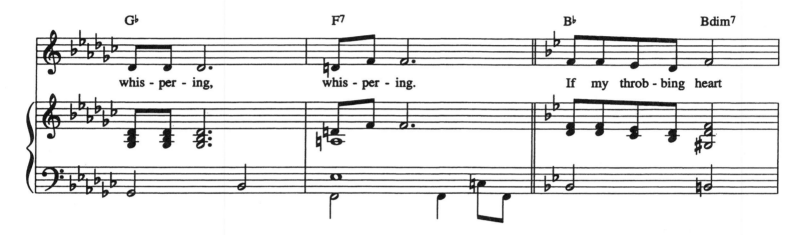

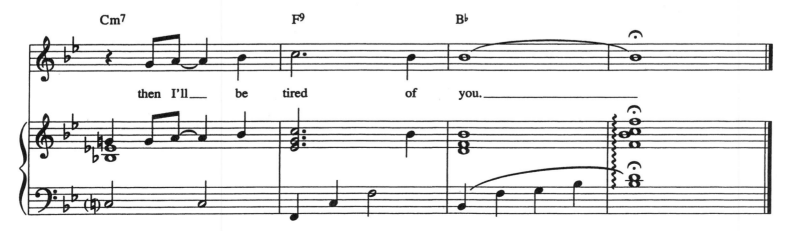

WHEN THE IDLE POOR BECOME THE IDLE RICH

Lyric by E.Y. "YIP" HARBURG
Music by BURTON LANE

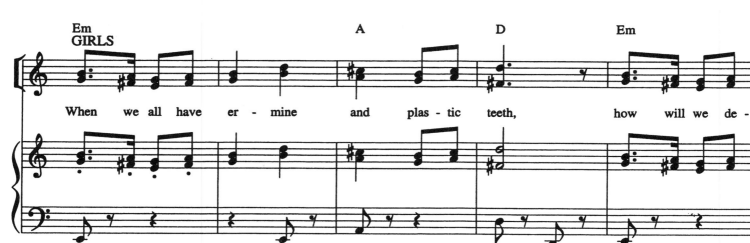

Em   A   D   Em
GIRLS

When we all have er - mine and plas - tic teeth, how will we de -

A   D   Dm   G
MEN

ter - mine who's who un - der - neath? And when all your neigh - bors are up - per

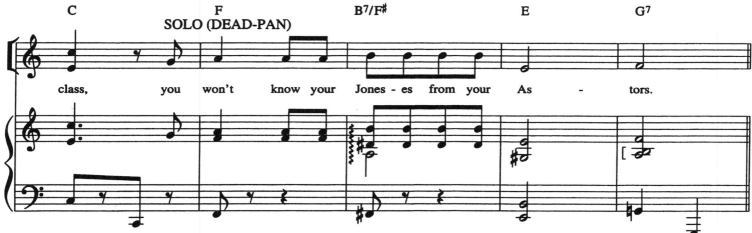

C   F   B7/F♯   E   G7
SOLO (DEAD-PAN)

class, you won't know your Jones - es from your As - tors.

C   C6(♭5)   C   C6(♭5)
SHARON

Let's toast the day, the day we drink that drink - ie up, but with the lit - tle

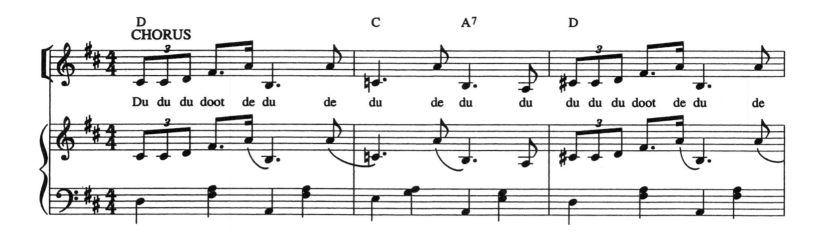

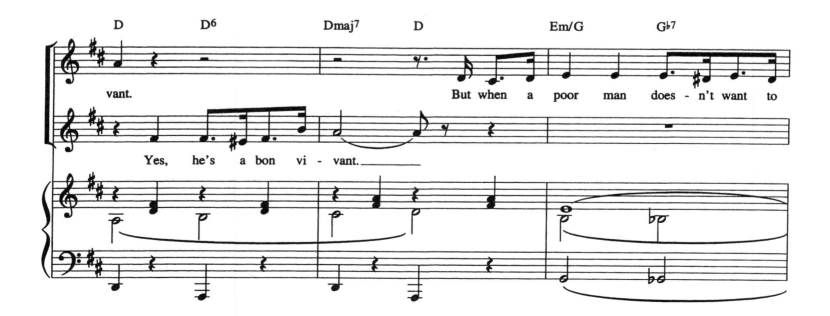

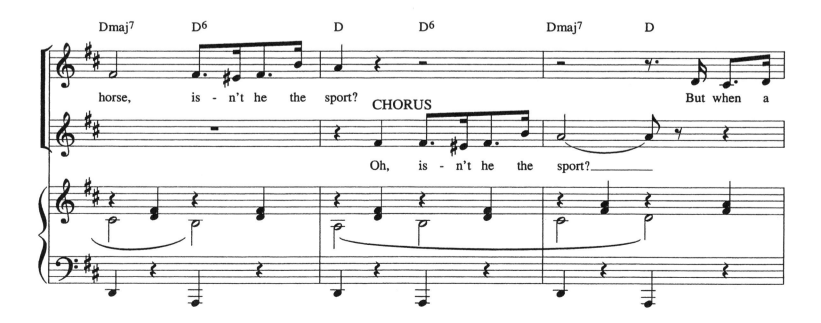

town. _____ But when a poor man cha - ses af - ter dames, he's a

bound - er, he's a round - er, he's a rot - ter, and a lot of dir - ty names.

CHORUS

Du du du doot de du de du de du du du du du doot de du de du de doot. You'll

When the i-dle poor, be-come the i-dle rich, you'll

nev-er know just who is who or who is which.

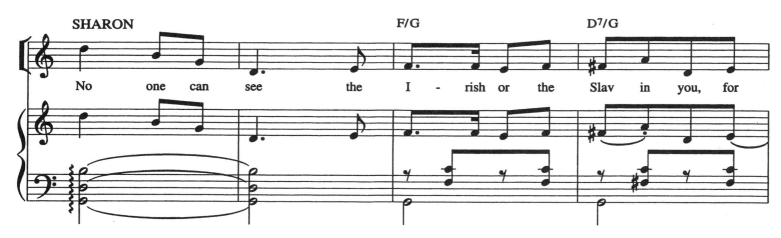

No one can see the I-rish or the Slav in you, for

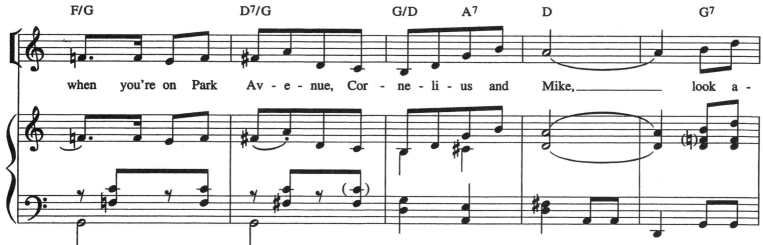

when you're on Park Av-e-nue, Cor-ne-li-us and Mike,_____ look a-

WE'RE OFF TO SEE THE WIZARD

Lyric by E.Y. "YIP" HARBURG
Music by HAROLD ARLEN

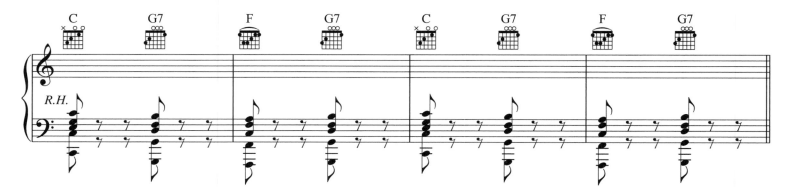

Fol - low the yel - low brick road, _____ fol - low the yel - low brick road, _____

fol - low, fol - low, fol - low, fol - low, fol - low the yel - low brick road. _____

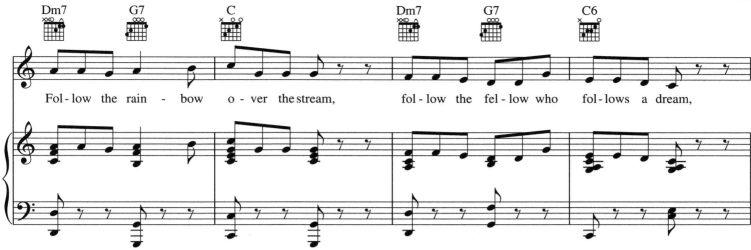

Fol - low the rain - bow o - ver the stream, fol - low the fel - low who fol - lows a dream,

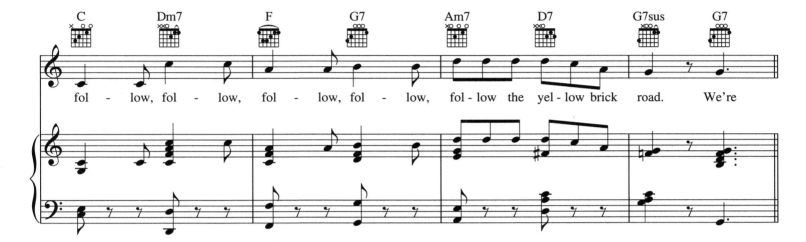

fol - low, fol - low, fol - low, fol - low, fol - low the yel - low brick road. We're

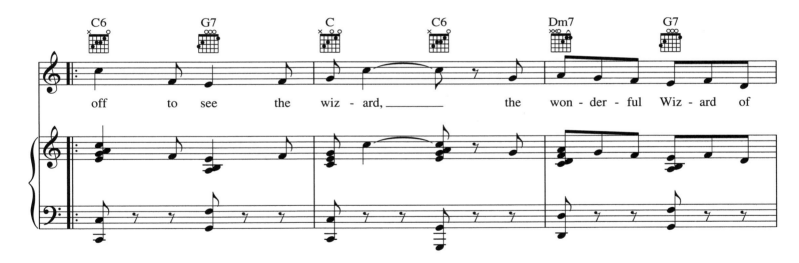

off to see the wiz - ard, _____ the won - der - ful Wiz - ard of

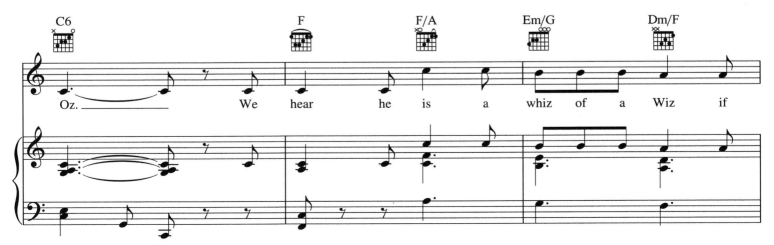

Oz. _____ We hear he is a whiz of a Wiz if

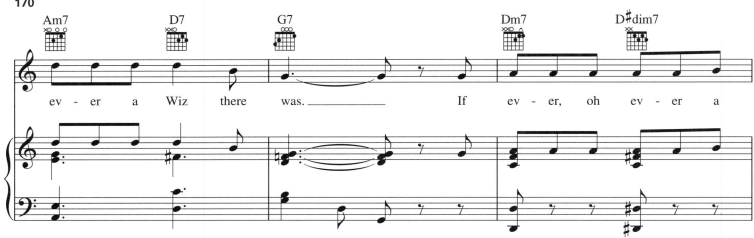

ev-er a Wiz there was. _____ If ev-er, oh ev-er a

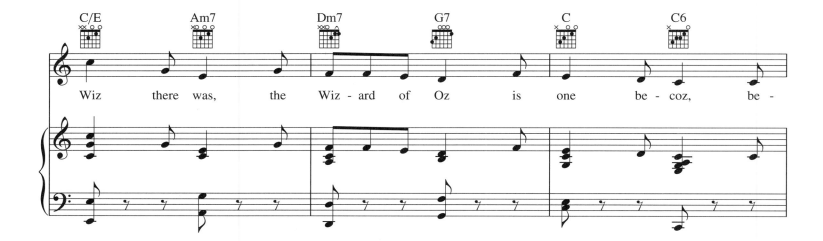

Wiz there was, the Wiz-ard of Oz is one be-coz, be-

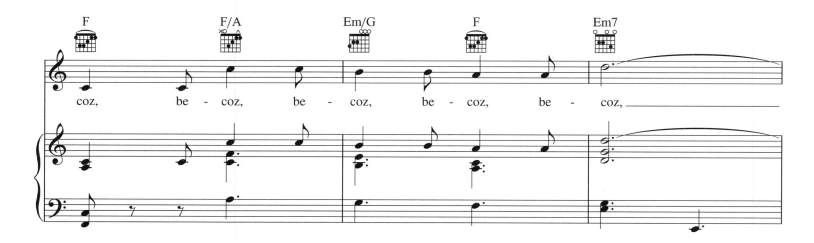

coz, be - coz, be - coz, be - coz, be - coz, _____

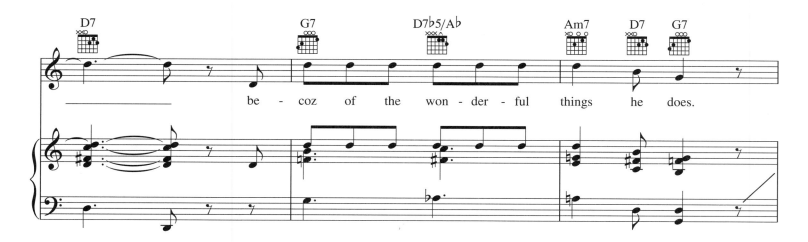

be - coz of the won-der-ful things he does.

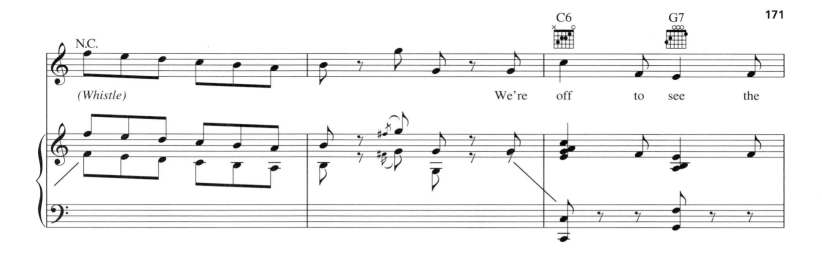

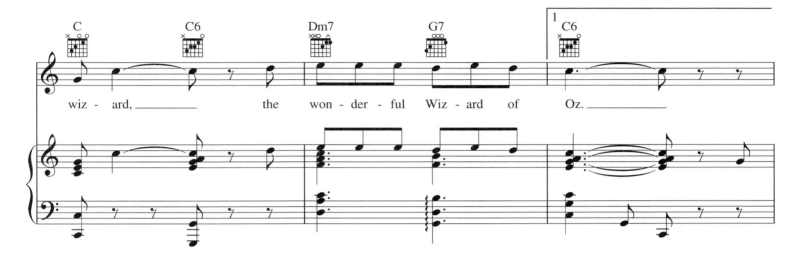

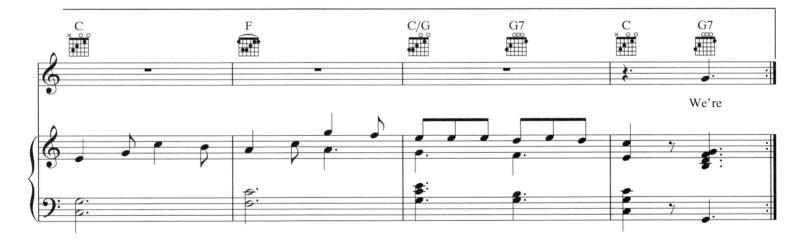

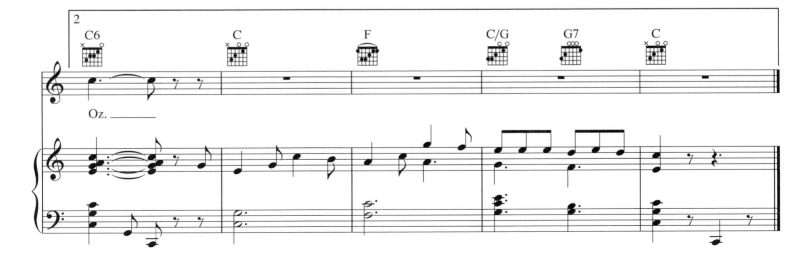

WHEN I'M NOT NEAR THE GIRL I LOVE

from FINIAN'S RAINBOW

Lyric by E.Y. "YIP" HARBURG
Music by BURTON LANE

Moderately, in 1

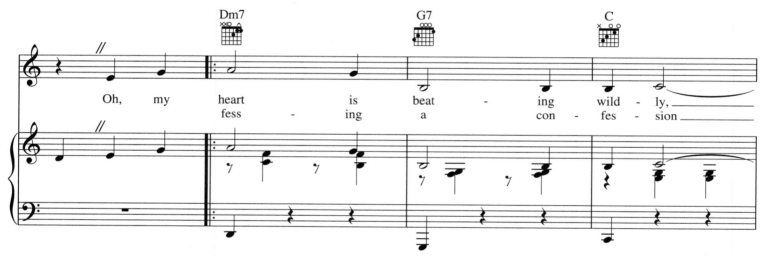

Oh, my heart is beat - ing wild - ly, _____ and it's all be - cause you're here.

fess - ing a con - fes - sion _____ and I hope I'm not ver - bose.